W9-BFE-742

Life in
Ancient Egypt

Other titles in the *Living History* series include:

Life in Ancient Egypt

Don Nardo

San Diego, CA

© 2015 ReferencePoint Press, Inc.
Printed in the United States

For more information, contact:
ReferencePoint Press, Inc.
PO Box 27779
San Diego, CA 92198
www.ReferencePointPress.com

LIBRARY OF CONGRESS CATALOGING-IN-PUBLICATION DATA

Nardo, Don, 1947-
    Life in ancient Egypt / by Don Nardo.
        pages cm. -- (Living history series)
    Includes bibliographical references and index.
    ISBN-13: 978-1-60152-638-0 (hardback)
    ISBN-10: 1-60152-638-5 (hardback)
 1. Egypt--Civilization--To 332 B.C.--Juvenile literature. I. Title.
    DT61.N327   2014
    932'.01--dc23
                                                                          2013040143

Contents

Foreword

Histroy is a complex and multifaceted discipline that embraces many different areas of human activity. Given the expansive possibilities for the study of history, it is significant that since the advent of formal writing in the Ancient Near East over six thousand years ago, the contents of most nonfiction historical literature have been overwhelmingly limited to politics, religion, warfare, and diplomacy.

Beginning in the 1960s, however, the focus of many historical works experienced a substantive change worldwide. This change resulted from the efforts and influence of an ever-increasing number of progressive contemporary historians who were entering the halls of academia. This new breed of academician, soon accompanied by many popular writers, argued for a major revision of the study of history, one in which the past would be presented from the ground up. What this meant was that the needs, wants, and thinking of ordinary people should and would become an integral part of the human record. As British historian Mary Fulbrook wrote in her 2005 book, *The People's State: East German Society from Hitler to Honecker,* students should be able to view "history with the people put back in." This approach to understanding the lives and times of people of the past has come to be known as social history. According to contemporary social historians, national and international affairs should be viewed not only from the perspective of those empowered to create policy but also through the eyes of those over whom power is exercised.

The American historian and best-selling author, Louis "Studs" Terkel, was one of the pioneers in the field of social history. He is best remembered for his oral histories, which were firsthand accounts of everyday life drawn from the recollections of interviewees who lived during pivotal events or periods in history. Terkel's first book, *Division Street America* (published in 1967), focuses on urban living in and around Chicago and is a compilation of seventy interviews of immigrants and native-born Americans. It was followed by several other oral histories including *Hard Times* (the 1930s depression), *Working* (people's feelings about their jobs), and his 1985 Pulitzer Prize–winning *The Good War* (about life in America before, during, and after World War II).

In keeping with contemporary efforts to present history by people and about people, ReferencePoint's *Living History* series offers students a journey through recorded history as recounted by those who lived it. While modern sources such as those found in *The Good War* and on radio and TV interviews are readily available, those dating to earlier periods in history are scarcer and often more obscure the further back in time one investigates. These important primary sources are there nonetheless waiting to be discovered in literary formats such as posters, letters, and diaries, and in artifacts such as vases, coins, and tombstones. And they are also found in places as varied as ancient Mesopotamia, Charles Dickens's England, and Nazi concentration camps. The *Living History* series uncovers these and other available sources as they relate the "living history" of real people to their student readers.

Important Events

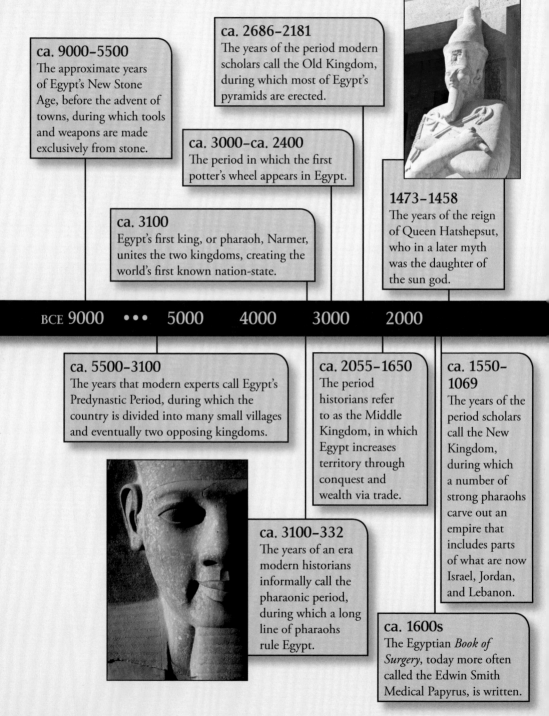

ca. 9000–5500
The approximate years of Egypt's New Stone Age, before the advent of towns, during which tools and weapons are made exclusively from stone.

ca. 2686–2181
The years of the period modern scholars call the Old Kingdom, during which most of Egypt's pyramids are erected.

ca. 3000–ca. 2400
The period in which the first potter's wheel appears in Egypt.

ca. 3100
Egypt's first king, or pharaoh, Narmer, unites the two kingdoms, creating the world's first known nation-state.

1473–1458
The years of the reign of Queen Hatshepsut, who in a later myth was the daughter of the sun god.

BCE 9000 • • • 5000 4000 3000 2000

ca. 5500–3100
The years that modern experts call Egypt's Predynastic Period, during which the country is divided into many small villages and eventually two opposing kingdoms.

ca. 2055–1650
The period historians refer to as the Middle Kingdom, in which Egypt increases territory through conquest and wealth via trade.

ca. 1550–1069
The years of the period scholars call the New Kingdom, during which a number of strong pharaohs carve out an empire that includes parts of what are now Israel, Jordan, and Lebanon.

ca. 3100–332
The years of an era modern historians informally call the pharaonic period, during which a long line of pharaohs rule Egypt.

ca. 1600s
The Egyptian *Book of Surgery*, today more often called the Edwin Smith Medical Papyrus, is written.

in Ancient Egypt

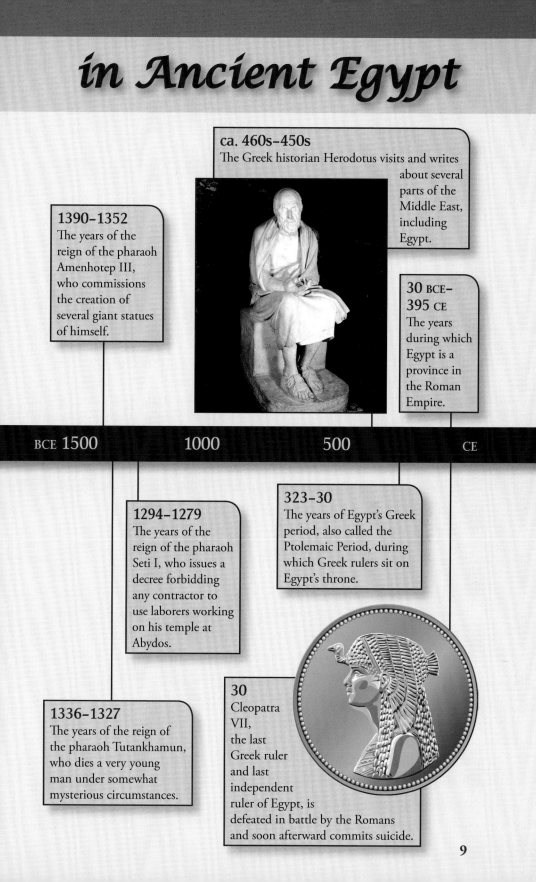

ca. 460s–450s
The Greek historian Herodotus visits and writes about several parts of the Middle East, including Egypt.

1390–1352
The years of the reign of the pharaoh Amenhotep III, who commissions the creation of several giant statues of himself.

30 BCE–395 CE
The years during which Egypt is a province in the Roman Empire.

BCE **1500**   **1000**   **500**   CE

1294–1279
The years of the reign of the pharaoh Seti I, who issues a decree forbidding any contractor to use laborers working on his temple at Abydos.

323–30
The years of Egypt's Greek period, also called the Ptolemaic Period, during which Greek rulers sit on Egypt's throne.

1336–1327
The years of the reign of the pharaoh Tutankhamun, who dies a very young man under somewhat mysterious circumstances.

30
Cleopatra VII, the last Greek ruler and last independent ruler of Egypt, is defeated in battle by the Romans and soon afterward commits suicide.

People of Extraordinary Devotion

Sometime in the 460s BCE, a young Greek man named Herodotus set out on the first of what would prove to be many long journeys. He visited Persia, encompassing what are now Iran and Iraq, along with many other parts of the known world of his era. In each place, he visited the major tourist sites. An individual with seemingly insatiable curiosity, he also studied the local customs and interviewed people of all walks of life, trying to get a handle on their beliefs, habits, and histories. All of this data, and more, eventually ended up in a long book. Titled *The Histories*, it is believed to be the first true history text ever written.

One of Herodotus's most adventurous and fascinating trips was the one he made to Egypt. In fact, he devoted considerably more space in his book to that foreign nation than he did to any other. After describing the country's geography, he said, "About Egypt I shall have a great deal more to relate because of the number of remarkable things which the country contains." On the one hand, Egypt had more huge structures that "beggar description than anywhere else in the world." These included gigantic statues of the kings, called pharaohs, and the enormous pyramids at Giza, built to house the bodies of those rulers. On the other hand, Herodotus continued, "the Egyptians themselves in their manners and customs"[1] were highly unusual and worthy of study.

The Most Religious People

Of those manners and customs, what captivated the wandering Greek more than any other was the lofty level of religious faith the Egyptians displayed. Indeed, in his words, "they are religious to excess, beyond any other nation in the world."[2] He then listed numerous spiritual rituals and habits the people practiced, often on a daily basis. These ranged from priests shaving their heads and bodies each day to ordinary folk drinking from special brass cups and carefully washing them daily in deference to the gods.

Herodotus was merely the first known scholar to have studied and written about ancient Egyptian religion. Historians down through the ages, including modern ones, have done the same. For example, as the late New York University professor Lionel Casson, a leading expert on ancient times, stated:

> Westerners place religion in a compartment of its own, separating it from other aspects of their existence. To an Egyptian, this would have been unthinkable. Religion permeated his whole life—socially, politically, and economically. As he saw it, every detail of his own life and of the life around him—from the predictable flooding of the Nile to the chance death of a cat—depended entirely on the attitude of the gods.[3]

The images of these gods and their various wondrous powers were based in part on natural forces and phenomena that the early Egyptians saw around them. Each force came to be represented by one or more specific gods. There was a deity who caused the annual Nile floods, for instance, along with gods associated with storms, the sun's rising and setting, the behaviors of animals, and the patterns of stars in the night sky. In this way the average Egyptian envisioned that he or she was completely surrounded, as well as constantly watched, by invisible superbeings.

WORDS IN CONTEXT

grave goods

Everyday objects placed in a tomb or grave, usually for the use of the deceased in the afterlife.

An Immortal Civilization

The concept of diverse gods controlling the natural world that encircled humanity is only one example of religious beliefs pervading all levels of Egyptian life. On a more down-to-earth, practical level, for example,

religious practices strongly affected Egypt's economy. People grew crops and made bread and wine not only for themselves, but also for offerings to the gods. Each and every day, countless tons of foodstuffs and drinks were employed in religious sacrifices in temples, tombs, homes, and elsewhere. Moreover, much of the wood imported at great expense into the country was used to create temple doors, coffins, and other objects associated with religion.

In addition, the religious temples in Egypt were in some ways like major modern corporations. They owned and operated vast farming estates, workshops, mines, and other enterprises that employed tens of thousands of people. Still more untold thousands of Egyptians were involved in the construction of the many huge structures that Herodotus mentioned. The majority of these monuments—including pyramids, temples, and towering statues of gods—were religious in nature.

Pyramids were used mostly as tombs—launching pads from which the souls of noble individuals could reach the afterlife. The Egyptians filled those tombs with all manner of grave goods, objects they expected to be used by the deceased in the next life. Likewise, over time the poor, who made up a majority of the populace, also became fixated on making it to the afterlife and devoted whatever time and energy they could to preparing themselves for an existence beyond the grave. "Even the poorest Egyptian burials," Casson remarked, "show some attempt to equip the deceased for the afterlife, though the equipment might consist of no more than a few scraps of food."[4]

> **WORDS IN CONTEXT**
> **religiosity**
> The degree of religious devotion possessed or displayed by a person or group.

At every turn, therefore, the people of ancient Egypt were confronted with or acted in accordance with religious ideas and obligations. In Egyptologist Rosalie David's words:

> The economy and industry of the country were inseparable from the religion. And unlike other societies, where they were organized for the sole benefit of the living and the state, in Egypt production of goods was specifically directed first toward the gods and the dead (so that they could enjoy eternal life) and only secondly attempted to provide a good standard of living for the people.[5]

As it turned out, this intense preoccupation with religion ultimately made the memory of ancient Egyptian civilization as immortal as the typical Egyptian hoped he himself would become. The extreme religiosity of everyone in the country, including their shared belief in a single, specific group of gods and articles of faith, helped to cement Egyptians of all walks of life—rich and poor—into a strong national unit. This was a major factor contributing to their nation's unusual longevity—more than three thousand years. In turn, that long existence gave the Egyptians ample time to create a multitude of impressive monuments and artifacts. These have fascinated and inspired every subsequent human generation, right up to the present, so that in a very real sense the spirit of ancient Egypt still thrives.

Chapter One

Houses and Home Life

Almost nothing is known for sure about the houses or any other aspects of the daily lives of the first inhabitants of what is now Egypt. This is mainly because they lived so long ago. It has been more than fifty thousand years since humans first occupied the extremely fertile banks of the Nile River. That mighty waterway—with a total length of 4,130 miles (6,646 km)—flows from south to north, dividing Egypt roughly in half. The river also gently overflows its banks once each year, laying down a layer of mud that encourages lush plant growth. The Egyptians later came to call this annual flooding event the inundation.

Those earliest arrivals in the region appear to have been hunter-gatherers, individuals who supported themselves by hunting, fishing, and gathering berries and other edible wild plants. Not until about 6000 BCE or so, roughly eight thousand years ago, did the Nile Valley's residents begin practicing agriculture. Modern experts think their homes were built from easily available natural materials such as bundled river reeds and bricks made from mud or clay. Because such substances are perishable, those structures disappeared long ago.

The estimation that reeds and mud were used for these primitive homes is based on the fact that the Egyptians were highly traditional. With very few exceptions, they maintained the beliefs, customs, and building methods of their ancestors. Indeed, at the height of Egypt's ancient culture in the 2000s and 1000s BCE, a majority of poor and rich folk alike used the same materials—reeds and/or mud bricks—to fashion their houses. Although most of those dwellings, too, have disintegrated, archaeologists have unearthed the crumbling remains of a few of them. Also, several paintings and pottery models of typical homes from the era have survived to confirm the age-old house-building methods of the region.

An Egyptian Watershed

The long time span that began with the ascendancy of Egypt's first pharaoh, Narmer (or Menes), in about 3100 BCE and ended with the country's takeover by Greek rulers in 332 BCE is often called the pharaonic period. Narmer's rule at the beginning of this period was a crucial watershed in Egyptian history. For an undetermined number of centuries before his time, the region had been widely disunited. At first it was divided into hundreds of small, independent villages; then a few dozen groups of villages, called nomes, formed; and finally, some divergent groups of nomes came together, creating two large, opposing kingdoms. One kingdom was in the south, or Upper Egypt, and the other was in the north, or Lower Egypt. (The Egyptians viewed the direction of the Nile's source, now seen as south, as north, and the direction of its flow, now viewed as north, as south.)

When Narmer, a king of the southern kingdom, came to power he completed the ongoing unification process. He brought the two lands together, forming the world's first true nation-state, and established a new capital, Memphis, near the old border between the once rival kingdoms. Later generations viewed Narmer as the country's first pharaoh. That word is a Greek version of the Egyptian term *per-ao* (or *per-aa*), meaning "great house."

The King's Palace

Narmer and the pharaohs who succeeded him certainly did live in a large and magnificent house. Literally a palace, it was by far the biggest home in the land. In fact, each pharaoh customarily had several palaces in various sectors of the country, in part so that he could visit those areas whenever he desired. Another reason for a single king to have multiple palaces was to ensure "that the royal power was represented in all the parts of the country,"[6] writes May Mohamed, a scholar at Minufeya University in northern Egypt.

In Their Own Words

Special Honors for a Pet

In addition to beds, chests, stools, oil lamps, and other common furnishings, many ancient Egyptian homes featured *living* belongings in the form of pets. Among those that have been documented are ferrets, monkeys, ducks, geese, and falcons. But as remains true across the world today, the most popular pets in Egypt were dogs and cats. Personal relationships between dogs and their owners were particularly strong, and families of all classes enacted open displays of grief when their dogs died. The Greek historian Herodotus confirmed this after visiting Egypt, writing that "when a dog dies they shave their whole body, including their head." Even more impressive were the honors accorded to a greyhound named Abuwtiyuw, who lived and died sometime in the mid-second millennium BCE. Apparently his owner was a pharaoh's bodyguard who brought the dog with him to work each day. The pharaoh came to know and love Abuwtiyuw, as proved by an inscription found by archaeologists at Giza, near modern Cairo. It reads:

> The dog which was the guard of His Majesty, Abuwtiyuw is his name. His Majesty ordered that he be buried, that he be given a coffin from the royal treasury, fine linen in great quantity, [and] incense. His Majesty gave perfumed ointment and ordered that a tomb be built for him by the gang of masons. His Majesty did this for him in order that he might be honored.

Herodotus, *The Histories*, trans. Aubrey de Sélincourt. New York: Penguin, 1978, p. 155.
G.A. Reisner, "The Dog Which Was Honored by the King of Upper and Lower Egypt," *Bulletin of the Museum of Fine Arts*, vol. 34, December 1936, p. 97.

Today only scanty remnants of some of those many palaces survive. For the most part, moreover, the bulk of these remains consist of audience halls, or throne rooms, where rulers greeted nobles, members of the general public, and foreign ambassadors. Some sections of these halls still exist, largely because they were made of stone, which is resistant to decay and the ravages of time.

In comparison, the residential portions of the palaces, where the pharaohs and their families actually dwelled, were composed mainly of impermanent materials, including bricks, wood, and plaster. So they are mostly gone. "Like all places of the living" in ancient Egypt, Mohamed says, "the king's residence was normally built of mudbrick with possibly some main doorways of stone. The walls, floors and ceilings were plastered and often painted, and columns and windows were of wood." She adds that "the buildings had for the most part only one story with possibly some galleries," or overhanging balconies, "as well as stairs to the roof."[7]

Homes of the Nobles

The nobles who socialized with the pharaoh and other well-to-do Egyptians had houses that were physically similar to the royal residences, only smaller. Most of these homes were townhouses, or city dwellings. An average example featured one, or more often two, stories and a dozen or more rooms that had diverse functions. If there were two floors, the first-story rooms usually consisted of a kitchen; one or more storerooms for food, cleaning materials, and other household items; workrooms where family members or people employed by the family made clothes, ground grain into flour, baked bread and pastries, and so forth; and rooms for dining and entertaining guests.

One or more wooden or brick stairways led to the family bedrooms on the upper story. "A rooftop terrace," Brooklyn Museum scholar James F. Romano writes, "afforded family members a place of nighttime refuge, where they could enjoy the delightful breezes blowing off the desert."[8]

Several members of Egypt's wealthy class also had country houses.

Sheltered from the difficulties of daily life in ancient Egypt, children from a wealthy family play in the garden of their country estate. Most such estates included vegetable and flower gardens, fruit orchards, fish ponds, and a variety of livestock.

Typically such a villa was enclosed and protected by a tall wall made of bricks or stone. Inside those walls was the family's private little oasis of comfort and safety, tucked neatly away from life's difficulties and uncertainties. In addition to bedrooms, a kitchen, dining areas, and workrooms, the household and its grounds had both vegetable and flower gardens; often little orchards with fruit trees and artificial ponds stocked with fish; pens and stables for goats, geese, donkeys, and other animals; and barns, granaries, and servants' quarters. With such a wide array of features and conveniences, a wealthy country house was an economic unit that could carry on from day to day and year to year more or less on its own.

The Convenience of Bathrooms

Whether it was located inside or outside a city, a well-to-do ancient Egyptian house had another crucial comfort that was absent from most other homes—one or more bathrooms. These lacked modern-style plumbing. So they were primitive by today's standards. Yet compared with what the average Egyptian was used to, such rooms were, in Romano's words, "elaborate bathing and lavatory facilities." A typical example

> consisted of a low mud-brick wall sheathed in limestone, with a limestone floor. The bather stood on this floor while attendants poured water over his or her body. Animal or vegetable oils mixed with powdered limestone served as cleansing agents. Excess water flowed into a pottery vessel that was emptied after bathing. A typical Egyptian latrine [toilet] was composed of a wood, clay, or in the wealthiest households limestone toilet seat that rested on a partially sand-filled pot.[9]

Every day or two, a servant emptied the pot, cleaned it, and poured in fresh sand.

In contrast, noted scholar of ancient Egypt Eugen Strouhal quips, "Most common people never saw a bathroom in their lives."[10] Instead, when average people needed to relieve themselves, they walked to a private corner of their home and used a portable pottery container, not unlike a modern bedpan. They then went outside and emptied the container.

Herodotus provided another, more graphic detail about local toilet habits. Egyptian women "pass water standing up," he said, while the men urinated sitting down. They always did it indoors, based on the theory "that what is unseemly but necessary should be done in private."[11] (The reason Herodotus found this preference for privacy odd is that in his native land of Greece, public toilets that lacked any sort of privacy were the norm.)

Lack of bathrooms among poorer Egyptians did not hinder their bathing habits. In fact, evidence clearly shows that Egyptians of all classes were extremely concerned with cleanliness. The average person eliminated this concern by frequently taking what is today called a sponge bath. This required filling a jug or other container with river water and carrying it indoors to a bedroom or other private space. People then wet a cloth and scrubbed themselves and/or "poured water over their hands and other body parts and caught it in a wide, deep bowl,"[12] Strouhal says. Archaeologists discovered one of these bathing bowls bearing the words "Good health to you when you wash your face, and let your heart rejoice!"[13]

Homes of Modest Means

Bathrooms were not the only conveniences that poorer homes lacked. They had considerably fewer rooms of any kind compared with well-to-do houses. A typical lower-class townhouse had three or four small rooms, with dirt floors and walls made of sun-dried mud bricks that crumbled rapidly and required frequent repairs.

Yet just as they overcame their scarcity of bathing facilities, many average homeowners found ways to make their tiny homes comfortable

Women fill jugs with water from the Nile River for use in bathing, cooking, and drinking. Evidence from ancient Egypt shows that people from all social classes valued cleanliness.

by decorating them as best as they could. It was common, for instance, to cover a dirt floor with a soft, clean mat made of woven river reeds. Also, according to British Museum scholar T.G.H. James, surviving "traces of paint show that the principal rooms were not only partly whitewashed, but also decorated with colorful paintings,"[14] along with pottery figurines of gods and other simple but attractive ornaments.

Moreover, James continues, "a house always looks better when it is furnished." The furniture in these houses, he says, "may very generally be classified under four headings: pieces to sit on, pieces to lie on, pieces to put things in, and pieces to put things on. Of the pieces to sit on, the most common throughout Egyptian history were stools, i.e. chairs without backs."[15]

The things to lie on consisted mainly of beds made of reed mats or a makeshift wooden frame supporting a mattress stuffed with reeds or straw. Typically there was a low wooden table for meals and/or to put things on. There were also one or more wooden chests for storing clothes and various other belongings. (Closets had not yet been invented.)

Another amenity that many Egyptians, including poorer ones, craved was a home garden. Even the humblest houses in ancient Egypt "had little gardens next to them," Strouhal writes. "Where buildings were close together, the owners might have to be content with a few trees or flower-beds, or simply grow flowers and small shrubs in clay pots or wooden troughs."[16]

Home Lighting

One thing these poorer homeowners had in common with their wealthy counterparts was that they all used the same means of lighting their houses. Windows, placed mostly high up in the walls, provided sufficient light in the daytime. These had no glass throughout most of Egypt's ancient centuries. Although the early Egyptians did make glass, it was opaque or translucent and used mainly for jewelry. Not until the country was under Roman rule (30 BCE–395 CE) did Egyptian glassmakers start making transparent glass and installing it in the windows of houses of the well-to-do.

At night, the main source of home lighting consisted of oil lamps. Their fuel came from palm fruit, olives, or other plants from which oils

Looking Back

Making Bread

In his classic book about ancient Egyptian life, the late renowned Egyptologist Adolf Erman explained how the ancient Egyptians made one of their principal food staples, bread. First, he said, someone used pieces of stone to grind the grain into flour, "in the same way as is done now in many parts of Africa." Then the person added water, sometimes along with milk, spices, salt, and eggs, to make the dough. The next step "in the making of bread" Erman continued,

> was the kneading of the dough, which could be done in different ways. Shepherds, in the fields at night, baking their cakes in the ashes, contented themselves with beating the dough in an earthen bowl and lightly baking their round flat cakes over the coals of the hearth. . . . [In a typical home] the dough was placed in a basket and kneaded carefully with the hands. The excess water was pressed out into a pot placed underneath the basket. The dough was then fashioned by hand into various shapes similar to those we now use for pastry, and these were baked on a conical stove. I purposely say *on* the stove, for the Egyptians seem to have been satisfied with sticking the cakes on the outside of the stove.

Adolf Erman, *Life in Ancient Egypt*, trans. H.M. Tirard. Charleston, SC: Nabu, 2010, pp. 190–91.

could be extracted. The most common sort of oil lamp then in use was a small bowl of oil in which the wick floated on the surface. More elaborate and decorative oil lamps, which often sat atop tall, ornamented stands, existed in the homes of the wealthy. Candles made from animal fat were also used for interior lighting in houses of both the rich and poor.

Whether they employed lamps or candles, a majority of Egyptians extinguished them considerably earlier in the evening than most people do today. On the one hand, there were no radios, televisions, video games, or other electronic devices to entertain families in their homes at the end of the day. On the other, the vast majority of Egyptians were illiterate, so reading was not a widespread leisure habit. In addition, age-old tradition had trained people to perceive daytime as a period of activity and nighttime as a period of inactivity. The result, says researcher André Dollinger, was that "mostly people went to bed when night fell and rose with the first light."[17]

One notable exception was an all-night religious festival that was particularly popular at Sais, in the Nile Delta. Herodotus witnessed it during his extended visit and later described it in his book, saying:

> On the night of the sacrifices everybody burns a great number of lights in the open air around the houses. The lamps they use are flat dishes filled with oil and salt, with a floating wick which keeps burning throughout the night. The festival is called the Festival of Lamps, and even Egyptians who cannot attend it mark the night of the sacrifice by lighting lamps, so that on that night lamps are burning, not in Sais only, but throughout the country.[18]

Common Foods

Besides sleeping, the most basic and repetitive daily activities in Egyptian homes were preparing and consuming the daily meals. The Egyptians practiced agriculture on a grand scale. So, as Romano remarks, they usually "had as much food to eat as they desired."[19] Of the many crops grown in the country, the most plentiful were varieties of wheat, with which the people made their staple food—bread (*te*). Evidence shows that the flour used to make it was most often coarse and grainy. In part, this is because the wheat was ground by stones with uneven surfaces, which left behind many partially crushed and uncrushed grains. By modern standards, therefore, Egyptian bread tended to be on the crunchy side.

The ovens employed to bake the bread came in different shapes and sizes. Overall the most popular version was a hollow pottery contraption that was roughly conical in shape and about 3 feet (1 m) high. A fire on the inside made the rounded sides hot, and when someone pressed a thin slab of dough onto the outer surface, it stuck there and baked. The surface of the oven was extensive enough to allow for baking several loaves at a time.

The Egyptians also consumed a lot of vegetables and fruits, along with some meat. Among the many vegetables were lentils, chickpeas, lettuce, turnips, beets, radishes, leeks, cucumbers, beans, garlic, and papyrus root (eaten mainly by the poor). Particularly popular were sweet onions. (People also placed onions in the armpits and eyesockets of mummies, believing that the sharp odor would allow the dead person's

spirit to breathe easier in the afterlife.) The fruits grown in Egypt during pharaonic times included dates, figs, grapes, plums, watermelons, coconuts (consumed mainly by the rich), and raisins. Only from the late 300s BCE on—when the Greeks and Romans controlled the country—were oranges, peaches, bananas, and lemons imported in significant numbers.

As might be expected, only wealthy households could afford meat on a regular basis. Most families of average means ate meat mainly on religious holidays and other special occasions. Numerous kinds of animals were bred or hunted for their meat in ancient Egypt, among them goats, sheep, cattle, desert gazelle and hares, birds (including geese, pigeons, ducks, heron, quails, and pelicans), and fish (including perch, mullet, tilapia, carp, catfish, and eel). Various types of meat, including certain fish, were eaten uncooked, while others were cooked, as confirmed by Herodotus. "Some kinds of fish they eat raw," he reported. They were "either dried in the sun or salted. Quails, too, they eat raw, and ducks and various small birds, after pickling them in brine. Other sorts of birds and fish, apart from those which they consider sacred, they either roast or boil."[20]

The typical Egyptian kitchen was stocked with spices and other substances that added to the flavor of both meats and vegetables, as well as the stews and other dishes that combined them. Among these additives were several that are common today. Salt was widely popular, for instance, as were coriander, cinnamon, fennel, dill, thyme, and mustard seeds. For sweeteners, rich folk could afford honey; in contrast, members of the lower classes used date juice, which they called *bener*, meaning "pleasant."

Cooking

Most Egyptian kitchens also featured various cooking oils. Archaeologists still debate whether butter was among them. But there is no doubt that animal fats, called *adj*, were popular, along with vegetable oils, known as *merhet*. The latter came from sesame and radish seeds, flax, horseradish trees, and castor-oil plants. Olive oil was long imported from Greece, Syria, and elsewhere until the Greek and Roman periods, when a thriving olive industry existed in the Faiyum region (about 80 miles, or 130 km, west of modern Cairo).

A common cooking custom was to pour some cooking oil into a wide pottery saucepan and add the food. The cook then suspended the pan over an open fire in a stone hearth or a conical oven like the kind used to bake bread. An alternative method employed in many upper-class homes was to place the food and oil in a metal brazier (a bowl-like vessel) and heat it over burning wood or charcoal.

In addition to saucepans, other common kitchen vessels included pottery mixing bowls and storage jars. The jars were frequently kept in small pantries. In wealthy households these could be small, separate chambers adjoining the kitchen, but in poorer homes they consisted of small spaces hollowed out below the kitchen floor. Among the more common kitchen utensils were wooden ladles, whisks, stirrers, and knives with blades of metal or sharpened stone.

Eating and Drinking

Some of the jars found in the kitchens of ancient Egyptian houses contained the culture's most popular beverages. Farm families that raised cattle and goats were the principal milk (*yatet*) drinkers, mainly because they had the easiest access to it when it was fresh. (There were no refrigerators, of course. So the milk tended to spoil before it could reach most city folk.) The residents of cities and the countryside alike drank large quantities of beer, however. Egyptian beer (*henqet*) was made from wheat and other grains and often seasoned with dates, spices, safflower, or other substances. Wine was another popular drink. More expensive than beer, it was found more often in wealthier homes, although the poor splurged and consumed it on special occasions.

People drank these beverages when they were thirsty. But the culture developed an array of stricter customs that revolved around food consumption. Among them were those that dictated the number of daily meals, which depended on one's social class. Families of average means tended to eat twice a day—a breakfast just before or after sunrise and a supper around sunset. Upper-class families, by contrast, also enjoyed hearty lunches.

Workers harvest a bountiful crop of wheat. Farming played a central role in Egyptian life, and wheat was one of the most important crops grown.

Dining Customs

Other dining customs varied according to a household's financial and social means. One was seating. Poorer individuals usually sat on the floor around a low table, whereas the wealthy more often used chairs, as most people do today. Also, in the rare situations in which a lower-class person dined with richer folk, he or she was expected to speak only when spoken to. A well-known moral adage warned, "If you are a guest at the table of one greater than you," make sure not to speak "to him until he bids you, for one knows not what may be offensive." Instead, talk only "when he addresses you."[21]

Still another way that mealtime in richer households differed from that in poorer ones was a strange custom that Herodotus witnessed during his stay in Egypt. "When the rich give a party and the meal is finished," he wrote, "a man carries round amongst the guests a wooden image of a corpse in a coffin, carved and painted to look as much like the real thing as possible, and anything from eighteen inches to three feet long. He shows it to each guest in turn, and says, 'Look upon this body as you drink and enjoy yourself. For you will be just like that when you are dead.'"[22]

> **WORDS IN CONTEXT**
> *henqet*
> Beer.

There was one dining ritual, however, that was the same in every Egyptian home, regardless of the owner's financial means and social status. Namely, no one used forks or spoons. "Eating utensils were very rare in ancient Egypt," Romano explains. "Even members of the royal family ate with their hands,"[23] a habit frequently portrayed in surviving wall paintings. Seen through modern eyes, this practice erases the supposed inequalities among ancient Egyptians, as well as those among modern peoples. It is a colorful reminder that, despite accidents of birth, ultimately no one is better than anyone else.

Chapter Two

Social Relationships and Duties

Everyone in ancient Egypt—rich or poor—had a set social status, or station, in life, along with an array of duties he or she was expected to perform. By far the richest and most famous and most influential individual in the country was the pharaoh. During the unified nation's first several centuries, he and his desires were supreme. Lionel Casson wrote, "All other Egyptians were his servants,"[24] and the government and religious temples claimed that he was a god who dwelled on Earth.

Over the course of several centuries, the pharaoh's absolute authority and divine image diminished in stature, and people viewed him only as a man. Yet he was a very wealthy and powerful one and always remained the nation's strongest and most esteemed figure. He and his family enjoyed lives of luxury, with palaces, large country estates, the finest clothes, and throngs of servants who catered to their every whim.

The Social Ladder

The pharaoh and his family occupied the top rung of a rigid social ladder. On the rung just below them sat a small group of nobles. Wealthy and privileged, they hobnobbed with each other, as well as with the king, and some of them served in various capacities in the government. Technically the pharaoh was the head of the government. But he did not run it on a regular basis. That job was performed by the vizier, or chief administrator, whose social rank was second only to the pharaoh's. The vizier oversaw the various government departments, among them those in charge of agriculture, granaries (grain stores), the army, large construction projects, and justice. Governors appointed by the pharaoh oversaw similar departments in their respective provinces. Most of the administrators who staffed both the national and provincial governments were literate and enjoyed respect and social status nearly as great as the nobles.

Also high in social rank were the priests who served in the temples. They and the reigning king were the only people allowed to enter the sacred inner chambers of those large structures. The priests not only maintained Egypt's ongoing relationship with the gods but also managed large rural estates that often employed thousands of people.

Some of those people were artisans, or skilled craftsmen, of various types. Along with successful merchants and military officers, they occupied the next rung downward on Egypt's social ladder. In a sense, they made up the country's middle class, which was tiny compared to the massive middle classes in modern industrialized nations like the United States.

The many others who toiled on the royal and temple estates, as well as on Egypt's countless small private farms, were peasants. These workers, who together made up an estimated 80 percent or more of the country's population, occupied the lowest rung on the social ladder. It was common for the members of peasant families to barely be able to feed themselves from month to month and year to year. However, they bore the burden of communal duties that were, by modern standards, way out of proportion to their low social status and state of poverty. They also paid hefty taxes, often in the form of crops. Indeed, the peasants were "responsible for providing the food, resources, and manpower for the whole country," Rosalie David explains. "Their work on the land was governed by the annual [Nile] inundation and the seasons, but they attempted through their arduous labors to produce enough food to satisfy their own limited needs. Through their taxes, they also fed the rest of the society and supplied the [food] offerings for the tombs and temples."[25]

WORDS IN CONTEXT

vizier

The chief administrator of ancient Egypt's government, second in authority only to the pharaoh.

Priests lead a procession from a temple. As the guardians of religion and the relationship between the people and their gods, the priests of ancient Egypt enjoyed both respect and wealth.

Women's Duties, Rights, and Jobs

With rare exceptions, a person born into the peasant class remained there, doing his duty to family and country without any realistic hope of bettering his position. Similarly, no matter which rung on the social ladder a family occupied, its members tended to bow to tradition and willingly follow the societal relationships and customs handed down from one generation to the next.

No one questioned or seriously protested that their society was patriarchal, or male dominated, for example. It was seen as perfectly normal that men should run the government, temples, courts, and other major institutions. Meanwhile, women, who had no political rights, were expected to manage the household, cook, make clothes, and most importantly, raise the children.

Beyond these general traditional roles and social restrictions, however, ancient Egyptian women enjoyed more personal freedoms and legal and economic rights than did women in most other ancient lands. For instance, Egyptian women were allowed to own, inherit, and hand down in their wills land and other kinds of property.

They could also enter into legally binding contracts, some examples of which have survived. In one instance, a woman named Taheb, whose husband had died, desired to build a house that would lie right alongside that of her neighbor. The law dictated that it was necessary to strike a deal with the neighbor and draw up a contract with him. That document states in part, "I am responsible to you if I build my house which forms the western boundary of your house." She went on to say she would "build my house from my southern wall to my northern wall up to your wall, provided that I do not insert any timber in it. And I shall lay my beams from south to north so that I may roof over the ground floor if I wish." In closing, she wrote, "If I fail to act accordingly to everything promised in the contract, I shall pay you five silver pieces." In contrast, "if you obstruct the building of my house, I shall do to you according to everything already mentioned, and I shall build my house without leaving for you a light-well [an open shaft in the roof of a building that allows light to enter]—without penalty."[26]

WORDS IN CONTEXT

patriarchal

Male dominated, as in a social/political system in which men have more rights and authority than women.

An Egyptian woman could also sue someone in court, a right that most ancient societies did not grant women. In one surviving case, after her husband's death a woman named Eset wanted to keep up the family's income by using the workrooms he had established near their home. But three male workers had taken over the rooms. "I am entitled to the workrooms of my husband Panakht," she told the judge. After considering the arguments from both sides, the judge decided in Eset's favor, declaring, "The woman is in the right. Let her husband's workrooms be given to her."[27]

Still another privilege Egyptian women benefited from was almost complete freedom of movement. (In comparison, an ancient Greek woman could not leave the house without a male escort, and even then she had to wear a veil.) This allowed large numbers of Egyptian peasant

In Their Own Words

My Husband the Freeloader!

Some Egyptian marriages ended in divorce for the same reasons they do today—infidelity, abuse, or other kinds of bad behavior by one or the other spouse. In this surviving letter, a married woman complains to her sister that her husband, Mery-Ma'at, has become a freeloader—a lazy person who avoids hard work and insists that his wife's relatives supply him with food and other necessities. She further reveals that he plans to cast her aside if she does not comply with his demands. His threat to send her "to the Black Land" means he might throw her out to fend for herself as a menial farm laborer. (The term *Black Land* referred to the dark, rich soil tilled by farmers, whose work was widely viewed as backbreaking and exhausting.)

> I will send this grain to you and you should have it ground for me and add emmer [wheat] to it and make it into bread for me, because I am quarreling with Mery-Ma'at. "I'll throw you out!" so he says, and he quarrels with my mother, [demanding she give him] grain for [his] bread. "Now, your mother does not do anything for you!" so he says to me, saying [also] "now, you have siblings, but they do not look after you!" So he says, arguing with me daily. "Now, look! . . . if you say something [argue], you will go down to the Black Land!"

Quoted in A.G. McDowell, *Village Life in Ancient Egypt*. New York: Oxford University Press, 1999, p. 42.

women to work outside the home. Some were employed in workshops that turned out cloth and/or clothes. Others labored on farms, planting and harvesting crops. Still others, Eugen Strouhal points out, worked "in temples as weavers, washerwomen, bakers, or millers."[28] Also, numerous poor women and slaves served as cooks and maids in upper-class households. In addition, some ancient documents mention women who worked in shops that sold wigs or cosmetics and even practiced medicine as doctors or their assistants.

Love and Marriage

Not all Egyptian women worked outside the home, however, and even those who did were expected to attend to their number one duty in both the family and society. This was to give birth to and raise children. That required having a husband, of course, and in most cases the manner in which women and men became couples was different than it is today.

Indeed, most marriages in Egypt were arranged. Usually a relative—most often a father, uncle, or grandfather—met with his counterpart in the other family and worked out an agreement in advance. Evidence suggests that only sometimes was the modern ideal of romantic love the basis of a marriage. Yet there is no doubt that some Egyptians did fall in love, since numerous love songs and poems, several of them beautifully written, have survived. This one, composed by a young man for his girlfriend, is typical: "My loved one is unique, without a peer, more beautiful than any other. See, she is like the star that rises on the horizon at the dawn of an auspicious year. She moves in a shimmer of perfection. Her complexion is superb. Her eyes are marvelously seductive. On her lips linger persuasive words. Never does she speak one word too many!"[29]

> **WORDS IN CONTEXT**
> *hemw*
> Exploited laborers in ancient Egypt who had certain basic civil rights and therefore were technically not slaves.

Those Egyptians who managed to find the sort of deeply felt love expressed by these words were likely in the minority. Yet most people aspired to find it. This is confirmed by the extensive use of magic spells intended to make one person fall in love with another. To the Egyptians, magic was viewed as a real natural force that was generated in some unknown way by the mysterious powers of one god or another.

Thus, in order for a spell to work, one had to call upon and request the aid of a particular deity. Archaeologists have found such spells written on pieces of broken pottery. In one, a man who desired to make a young woman fall madly in love with him invoked the help of Ra, god of the sun: "Grant that this girl, true child of her mother, pursue me with undying passion, follow close on my heels like a cow seeking pasture, like a nursemaid minding her charge, like a guardian after his herd! For if you will not cause her to love me, I must surely abandon the day, consumed to dust in the fire of my burning."[30]

Whether a bride and groom were in love or not, the average age at which Egyptian males got married was between fifteen and twenty. Females were a bit younger, most often twelve to fourteen. Once it was decided who would marry whom, the actual marriage process was very uncomplicated by modern standards. As May Mohamed puts it, "There was no legal or religious ceremony by which marriage was formalized, and marriage occurred when a man and a woman established a household together."[31] More often than not, however, the bride's and groom's families did get together to celebrate the union. Surviving wall paintings and writings describe wedding parties that involved feasting, singing, dancing, and storytelling.

Getting a Divorce

Evidence for how many ancient Egyptian marriages succeeded is lacking. What historians do know is that some of them ended in divorce, just as they do today. The reasons for breaking up also largely mirrored modern ones. Among others, they included adultery, spousal abuse, the wife's inability to bear children, and serious criminal activity by a husband or wife.

Of these causes of divorce in Egypt, adultery appears to have been the most common. In a majority of the known cases, the husband accused the wife, which may reflect the fact that the male-dominated society viewed a wife's infidelity as more disreputable and unforgivable than a husband's. Still, Egyptian literature does contain a number of warnings against male cheaters. One cautions, "Do not sleep with a wife who is not yours, that no fault may be found with you because of it."[32] In another

A statuette carved around 2475 BCE depicts a couple and their children. Although some women worked outside the home, raising children was considered the primary duty of ancient Egyptian women.

instance, a male construction worker named Amen-nakhte openly condemned another man in his village, one Pa-neb, of multiple infidelities: "Pa-neb slept with the lady Tuy when she was the wife of the workman

Qenna. Pa-neb slept with the lady Hel when she was with [her husband] Pen-dua. Pa-neb [also] slept with the lady Hel when she was with [her second husband] Hesy-su-neb-ef. [And] when he had slept with Hel, he slept with Webkhet, her daughter."[33]

The actual divorce process began with one spouse—usually, but not always, the one accused of cheating—leaving the house. A majority of ancient Egyptian homes were owned by men. So more often than not, the wife was expected to find lodgings elsewhere, perhaps with her parents or a sibling. In one documented case, a male friend of a husband who had thrown his wife out took her in for a while. Because she had nowhere else to go, the friend wrote, "His wife spent forty days dwelling with me in my house, and I provided for her."[34] The parties also had to sign a formal agreement that said, among other things, that one, the other, or both were free to remarry.

Children, Toys, and Games

Whether a husband and wife stayed together or got divorced, they usually produced at least a few children and frequently many. In fact, the societal ideal was to have as many as was physically and financially possible. To this end, they did not practice exposure—leaving unwanted infants outside to die—as did the Greeks, Romans, and many other ancient peoples. In his famous geography book, the first-century-BCE Greek traveler and writer Strabo said, "One of the customs most zealously observed among the Egyptians is this, that they rear every child that is born."[35] By this, Strabo meant every child that survived birth. Because of the primitive state of medical knowledge, poor sanitation, and other factors, infant mortality took a terrible toll in ancient societies, including Egypt. Modern estimates for the number of babies that died at or soon after birth range from 20 to 50 percent (compared with less than 1 percent in the United States and other advanced modern countries).

As in many cultures, children who survived the first years of life enjoyed playing with toys, many of which are still common today. This is known because archaeologists have found both paintings of them and full-fledged versions deposited in tombs. There were dolls of various types, for instance, including the paddle doll. Its body was a carved, painted wooden paddle, and the hair was fashioned from sun-dried clay wrapped around flax threads. Other common toys included wooden crocodiles with movable jaws; mice, cats, dogs, donkeys, hippos, and other animals made from wood, pottery, ivory, or bone; wooden balls and tops; and miniature swords, chariots, and other weapons.

WORDS IN CONTEXT
kenbet

In ancient Egypt, a local court in which the accuser and accused tried the cases themselves before a judge.

Children also enjoyed a wide range of games and other activities. Among the many ball games depicted in wall paintings was one in which teams of two children each were involved. One teammate carried the other piggyback while his or her companion threw a ball to the topmost player of a rival team. In addition, tug-of-war and an early version of hopscotch were popular, and boys eagerly took part in the ancient world's most popular sport—wrestling. Egyptian children of both genders, and adults as well, also played board games. The most widely admired one was *senet*, in which the players moved game pieces along a grid of squares similar to numerous modern board games.

The number of toys and games in a child's life was tied to his or her family's financial well-being. The offspring of the rich had ample time for play because they did not have to worry about work. In contrast, children from poor families had to work, often before they reached the age of ten. Boys helped with planting and harvesting or started to learn the father's trade, while girls aided their mothers in making clothes, cleaning, and cooking. Thus, a majority of Egyptians had much shorter childhoods than young people typically do today.

The Question of Slavery

Some Egyptian households included individuals known as *hemw* (HEM-oo). People in later ages who studied ancient Egypt assumed they were slaves. But they were very unlike the slaves in ancient Rome and pre–Civil War America. In those two notorious slave-owning societies, slaves possessed no civil or legal rights; could neither own property nor marry free persons; and could be abused or even murdered by their owners with few or no consequences.

By comparison, the Egyptian *hemw* had several fundamental rights. They could earn wages for their toils, for example. Also, they could own property, including land, and dispose of it as they desired. In addition, they were allowed to marry anyone they wanted, including free people. Thus, David insists, "there were no true slaves in ancient Egypt."[36]

That does not mean that the *hemw* were treated like everyone else, however. They worked long hours, they had to do whatever their masters ordered, and their movements were severely limited. Whatever these individuals are called, modern scholars generally agree that they had significantly fewer rights than other Egyptians.

In whatever manner one defines the *hemw*, they played a significant role in society, mainly because they were paid less than free workers. That allowed their masters to get certain menial tasks done more cheaply than would have been possible using free persons' labor. Well-to-do households and estates, like the royal palace, the mansions of nobles, and temple estates, used numerous *hemw*—probably thousands or even tens of thousands, although exact numbers are unknown. As for households of average means, not all kept *hemw*, and those that did used far fewer than did wealthy households. For homeowners who could barely afford to support their families, feeding, housing, and paying extra helpers was simply too expensive. Those average households that did keep *hemw* as maids and other servants likely had fewer than half a dozen.

There were several different ways that a person might become a *hem* (singular of *hemw*) in Egypt. During some eras, many originated as war captives. Evidence suggests that others were free people who became *hemw* to work off debts they owed. Also, it appears that they could be free people who committed crimes and lost some of their rights as a punishment, while at least some were born with fewer rights because their parents were *hemw*.

A Duty to Obey the Law

Like all members of a household, the *hemw* were expected to do their duties not only to the owner and his family, but also to society in general,

Looking Back

Popular Board Games

Although several boards and game pieces used in the ancient Egyptian board game *senet* have survived, its exact rules have not. To help make up for this shortfall, modern experts have made some educated guesses about the game's basic strategies. Noted historian Ian Shaw speculates about it, as well as describes what is known about another board game that was popular in ancient Egypt.

> The most popular board game known to the Egyptians was *senet*, the game of "passing," which was played either on elaborate inlaid boards or simply on grids of squares scratched on the surface of a stone. The two players each had an equal number of pieces, usually seven, distinguished by shape or color, and they played on a grid of thirty squares known as *perw* ("houses") and arranged in three rows of ten. Moves were determined by "throw-sticks" or knucklebones [dice-like pieces of wood or bone]. The object was to convey the pieces around a snaking track to the finish, via a number of specially marked squares representing good or bad fortune. . . . A less popular board game, "twenty squares," is thought to have been introduced from western Asia. Although several boards have survived, and it is known to have been played by two players using five pieces, the rules of the game, as with *senet*, have not been preserved.

Ian Shaw, "Games," in *The Dictionary of Ancient Egypt*, by Ian Shaw and Paul Nicholson. New York: Abrams, 1995, p. 107.

and without complaint. Indeed, beyond their expected duties in the domestic sphere, all Egyptians were expected to revere and worship the gods and to obey the pharaoh and his administrators. Furthermore, obeying those top officials entailed the added duty of following the laws they and/or the gods had set down.

The results of these attitudes were impressive by modern standards. Many historians conclude that, despite the existence of an undetermined number of assorted lawbreakers, overall the ancient Egyptians were an exceptionally law-abiding people. For the most part, they believed in equal treatment and justice for all. Moreover, they were convinced that the gods were watching them on a regular basis. So the vast majority of them respected one another and felt a duty to uphold social tradition and justice.

This can be seen in their active participation in the nation's justice system, which featured three kinds of court settings. The first was a local court, or *kenbet*, consisting of a group of officials or elders who acted as judges. Little is known about how the informal *kenbet* hearings worked. But it appears that there were no lawyers, and the litigants (accuser and accused) presented the evidence themselves. The judges expected them to be truthful and enforced this demand with stiff penalties for lying. The importance of honesty in court was emphasized in an adage in the *Instruction of Amenemope*, a document widely popular in Egypt in the late first millennium BCE. "Do not go to court and falsify your words," it says. Instead, one should "tell the truth before the judge, lest he lay a hand on you."[37] The phrase "lay a hand on" seems to suggest that someone who lied might receive some sort of beating.

Judgments Rendered

For the most part, local courts dealt with lower-level issues such as petty theft, assault, and disputes over land. More serious offenses such as murder were litigated in a court overseen by the pharaoh's vizier. There was also a third court involving temple priests, who in certain situations purported to ask a god to hand down a judgment about whether someone was guilty or innocent.

Whichever court setting was involved, those individuals who were found guilty faced punishments harsher that those imposed by most modern courts. Penalties for minor crimes included paying a fine, beating with a whip or large stick, forced labor for several months or a few years, or exile. More serious crimes incurred sentences such as cutting off noses, hands, or other body parts, and execution. The perpetrator of the worst crime of all in the eyes of many Egyptians—tomb robbing—was thrown alive to hungry crocodiles.

Most ancient Egyptians never suffered any of these punishments, because they stayed out of trouble and concentrated on fulfilling their duties to family, community, and country. In general, they envisioned that as long as they upheld those duties as good citizens, the gods would look kindly on them. In their minds, after all, it was the gods who had first created the concepts of good, evil, and justice and ordained that bad and unjust people should be punished and good people rewarded. A passage in a text from the third millennium BCE sums up this belief: "Justice is done to him who does what is loved," it reads, "and punishment to him who does what is hated. Thus life is given to the peaceful, death is given to the criminal."[38]

Chapter Three

Personal Care, Health, and Education

Although an Egyptian's duty to family and society occupied an important place in daily life, needs of a more personal nature also required regular attention. Egyptians of all classes valued cleanliness and grooming. This encompassed everyday customs like bathing and skin care; personal enhancements such as mouthwashes, perfumes, and cosmetics; clothing items of various kinds; and jewelry, worn by both women and men.

Personal health was also important. Staying healthy was a daunting challenge in an era in which germs and other causes of disease were unknown and much (though certainly not all) medical knowledge built on superstition and magic. Indeed, the vast majority of people believed in and to some degree relied on magic spells to heal themselves and others.

Still another important area of personal concern was education and learning. In contrast to most modern societies, the Egyptians had no public education system designed to prepare young people for work and other aspects of later life. Education was not only privately administrated but also highly selective. Only a fortunate few, mostly boys, had access to a decent education, and what was deemed decent then was extremely limited compared with even the most mundane course of studies today.

Personal Grooming

Of these various personal concerns, by far the most fundamental on a day-to-day basis was grooming. Evidence, including sculptures and images in paintings, indicates that even those of minimal means were very concerned with their personal appearance. To begin with, they put great store in cleanliness. Most people bathed daily, even if it was only a sponge bath. Washing one's face and hands both before and after eating every meal was also a widespread habit.

The Egyptians practiced several other daily hygiene rituals. One was using their equivalent of modern mouthwashes, an activity they dubbed *sen shem shem*, or "bathing the mouth and teeth." The most common cleansing substance they employed was natron, a mixture of mineral salts dissolved in water.

Skin care was also viewed as essential, in part because Egypt's weather was frequently sunny and hot and people received a lot of direct exposure to the sun's rays. They were also regularly subjected to tiny sand particles blown in from the expanses of desert lying just beyond the fertile regions bordering the Nile. To combat skin damage, they used lotions extracted from the fat of animals such as sheep, hippos, and crocodiles. Also popular were vegetable oils, such as those extracted from flax and castor beans.

Smelling good was also a pervasive concern. People associated personal odors, in particular pleasant ones, with the gods, whose bodies were said to be highly fragrant. Most Egyptians who lived in and after the late second millennium BCE were familiar with the tale of how the sun god supposedly impregnated the mother of Queen Hatshepsut (who reigned between 1473 and 1458 BCE). That deity, Ra, the story went, found the queen asleep in her bed and "she waked at the fragrance of the god, which she smelled in the presence of his majesty." As the two made love, the queen "rejoiced at the sight of his beauty, and his love passed into her limbs, which the fragrance of the god flooded [with] all his odors."[39]

Hoping to emulate the sweet-smelling gods, most Egyptians used deodorants and body rubs. The poor wiped on concoctions made from ground-up roots and herbs, while wealthier folk bought more expensive perfumes that were mostly made locally. In fact, Egypt became renowned for its fine perfumes, which in the first millennium BCE were exported to cities across the Mediterranean world. Egyptian perfumes and body rubs were made primarily from plants. According to André Dollinger, these included "the roots, blossoms, or leaves of henna, cinnamon, turpentine, iris, lilies, roses, bitter almonds, etc., [which] were soaked in oil and sometimes cooked. The essence was extracted by squeezing, and oil was added to produce liquid perfumes, while creams and salves were the result of adding wax or fat. Many perfumes had more than a dozen ingredients."[40]

Women—and quite a few men, too—also tried to look good by using makeup. To give the cheeks some extra color, one applied a powdered rouge made from iron oxide, or rust. By adding animal fat and/or tree resins to this powder, one created the most commonly used lipstick in

As depicted in this wall painting from ancient Egypt, men wore kilts or loincloths wrapped around their waists and women wore simple, tube-shaped dresses sewn along one side. Most clothing was made from linen, which came from the fibers of the flax plant.

ancient Egypt. Especially popular was eye makeup, of which the earliest known version was a green powder derived from malachite, a form of copper oxide. Black eyeliner, called *kohl*, was produced from assorted lead compounds. To apply the liner and other eye makeup, one wet a finger or a small stick with oil or water, dipped it into the powder, and gently rubbed it onto the skin.

Evolving Clothing Styles

One important aspect of personal appearance, clothing, denoted or showed off a person's status in Egyptian society. Elegant outfits were a clear sign of wealth and high social rank. Still, ordinary Egyptians made their own fashion statements by ensuring that their garments were well laundered. Unless a person was in the midst of performing a task that was expected to dirty the clothes, such as digging a ditch, it was considered a breach of good social manners to appear in public with soiled attire. This explains Herodotus's observation that the Egyptians "make a special point of continually washing"[41] their clothes.

Most ancient Egyptian clothes were made from linen, which came from the fibers of the flax plant. Clean linen garments were not only attractive in a basic way but also "light and cool to wear," in May Mohamed's words. She goes on to describe the main ways they were worn: "Garments were draped round the body rather than tailored, and sewing was kept to a minimum. The chief form of decoration was pleating, and from examples of garments which have survived it is clear that a mechanical process was used to put the small, regular pleats into the cloth and that some form of starch or siz[ing] was used to fix them."[42]

The styles of these garments evolved a bit over time, as confirmed by changes recorded in wall paintings and sculpted figurines, although the tradition-loving Egyptians rarely strayed from a few basic clothing types. Before the mid-second millennium BCE, farmers and general laborers most often wore a simple loincloth or apron. Soldiers, merchants, and most others donned a kilt consisting of a rectangular piece of cloth wrapped around the waist. Most often it hung to the knee. Women wore a dress that was effectively a cloth tube sewn up on one side of the body.

In Their Own Words

Respect for Scribes

The famous Egyptian document best known as the *Satire of Trades* dates from sometime between 2025 and 1700 BCE, during the period that modern historians call the Middle Kingdom. One passage emphasizes how scribes viewed their own profession—as the best and most fruitful in the land—and in the process calls attention to the importance of getting the finest education possible. "I have seen defeated men," the scribe who narrates the passage states, individuals who are hopeless because they are not educated. He goes on to stress that a person who aspires to become educated and a scribe "must give yourself whole-heartedly to learning" to read and write. In that way, he will

> discover what will save you from the drudgery of underlings. Nothing is so valuable as education. It is a bridge over troubled waters. Just read the end of the *Book of Kemyt*, where you will find these words: "A scribe in any position whatsoever at the royal palace will never be needy there." And unless he shares his wisdom with other persons, he can never leave this life contented. I do not see a calling equal to it and agree with what this wise book says. Let me urge you to love learning more than your mother and have its perfections enter your mind. It is more distinguished than any other occupation. There is nothing [else] like it upon Earth!

Quoted in John L. Foster, trans., *Ancient Egyptian Literature*. Austin: University of Texas Press, 2001, pp. 33–34.

After the mid-second millennium BCE, people of modest means continued to wear simple dresses, kilts, and loincloths. But members of the upper classes started sporting more elaborate combinations of garments. Males still wore kilts, but they had become more like undergarments. Over them men draped a thin linen tunic that hung below the knee. Many men also wore short-sleeved linen shirts instead of going bare-chested. Well-to-do women sometimes wore tunics, too, and their dresses became more ornamental, featuring fringes and other decorative touches. More than one thousand years later, in Egypt's Greek period, members of the upper classes adopted several Greek fashions, important among them the himation, a big cloak-like garment worn over a tunic or dress.

Some Egyptians of that era also adopted Greek-style hats, which had very wide brims to block the sun from people's foreheads and eyes. In prior ages, however, hats and other forms of headgear were uncommon. Many modern artistic depictions of ancient Egypt, particularly movies, incorrectly show Egyptians of all social levels wearing the *nemes*, a cloth headdress folded so that the sides flared outward (as seen from the front). In reality, it was worn almost exclusively by members of the Egyptian royal family and a handful of nobles.

Common Health Threats

Just as the average Egyptian wanted to *look* as good as possible, he or she also wanted to *feel* good. Injuries, illness, and disease were as common in Egypt as they were in all human societies before the advent of the germ theory of disease and the other major medical advances of the past two centuries. Moreover, ignorance of the causes of disease was not the only threat to good health in Egypt. Although as a people the Egyptians were unusually clean from a bodily standpoint, they frequently lived in conditions that are now known to be unsanitary.

Both overcrowding and poor ventilation were common in the tiny homes of the poor, for example. They regularly inhaled airborne germs and toxins, increasing the incidence of lung infections and diseases like tuberculosis. Meanwhile, flies spread disease far and wide. Those pesky insects carried bacteria from sewage to food, causing intestinal infections like typhoid fever. In fact, flies were so abundant that people often tended neither to notice them nor to swat them away. As a result, trachoma and other eye diseases spread by flies were far more common than they are today.

In addition, mosquitoes were rampant in marshy areas like the Nile Delta, so those regions witnessed frequent flare-ups of diseases like malaria. The inhabitants of such areas attempted to avoid the mosquitoes by erecting raised wooden structures on which to sleep at night. Herodotus saw them and claimed they worked fairly well because the

mosquitoes "are prevented by the wind from flying high." To supplement these makeshift platforms, he continued, each marsh resident "provides himself with a net, which during the day he uses for fishing, and at night fixes up round his bed and creeps in under it before he goes to sleep."[43]

Regarding those beds, Eugen Strouhal asserts that "Egyptian houses were also infested with bedbugs." Furthermore, living rooms, and especially storerooms and grain stores, "attracted rats, mice, and other troublesome rodents."[44] Indeed, archaeologists found rat holes in the corners of rooms in many excavated ancient houses. They also discovered numerous tiny rodent skeletons in the remains of houses built inside a large fortress in southern Egypt. In addition, Strouhal points out, one of the several rat species that infested Egypt was undoubtedly "the Black Rat, host to the *Xenopsylla cheopsis* flea that can carry the agent of bubonic plague."[45] This is the terrible disease that came to be called the "Black Death" in medieval Europe, where it killed many millions of people. A surviving document by an ancient Greek physician, Rufus of Ephesus, describes symptoms of a disease that struck ancient Egypt in the first century CE, and modern medical authorities are nearly certain it was bubonic plague.

Healing Through Magic

Whatever diseases the Egyptians faced, they diligently attempted to fight back. To that end, they employed a combination of healing methods, some of which were moderately effective, but others totally fruitless. The unsuccessful ones used various forms of *heka*, or magic, which was a fundamental element of Egyptian religious beliefs.

Indeed, believing wholeheartedly that magic was a real phenomenon, people of all walks of life wore or carried amulets. Amulets are objects thought to possess supernatural qualities that can protect the wearer from harm, including illness. Not only did magic supposedly help ward off disease, some Egyptian doctors employed magic spells they hoped would cure an ailment after it had struck someone. Several surviving Egyptian medical writings feature magic spells designed to rid the body of disease. Sometimes the doctor recited the spell himself, but quite often he instructed the patient to recite the words of the spell over and over until his or her symptoms disappeared.

One of the gods most frequently invoked in such spells was Isis, a widely revered fertility goddess. Typical is a spell that reads, "O Isis, you great enchantress, heal me, deliver me from all evil, bad typhonic [disastrous] things, from demoniacal and deadly diseases and pollutions of all sorts that rush upon me!"[46]

Another form of magical healing involved holy water, ordinary water that was thought to have gained special properties through the power of a god. To make a batch of holy water, a priest dripped river water over a god's sacred statue. The supposedly transformed liquid fell down into small pools. Sick people then bathed in such pools in hopes of being cured.

> **WORDS IN CONTEXT**
> *kohl*
> A kind of black eye liner made from lead compounds.

Accumulated Medical Knowledge

Some Egyptian doctors used magic exclusively to treat their patients. But others turned to herbal remedies and similar therapies in addition to magic. The remedies, which had been used for untold centuries, were employed mainly for aches and pains and other everyday, non-life-threatening problems. The physicians wrote down many of these traditional cures on papyrus rolls, some of which have survived. One, which modern experts call the Ebers Medical Papyrus, recommends several remedies for stomachaches, including these two:

> 1. Another remedy for the emptying of the belly and the removal of aches in the stomach of the man: Seeds of the castor-oil plant shall be chewed and washed down with beer, so that everything will come out which is in his stomach. 2. Another (remedy) for the removal of any illnesses of the stomach: Roasted figs shall be combined with Behen-oil, raisins likewise, [and] seeds of the *Snj-*fruit, likewise. They shall be mixed into a homogeneous [uniform] mass, [and] it shall be eaten by the man in whose stomach the illnesses are.[47]

A physician treats a patient who is suffering from lockjaw, better known in modern times as tetanus—a serious bacterial disease that affects the muscles and nerves. Some of the techniques used by ancient Egyptian doctors for treating injuries and wounds are similar to those used today.

Like all such remedies through the ages, some of those used in Egypt worked and others did not. More reliable and significant was the Egyptian medical establishment's accumulated knowledge about how to treat the serious wounds and injuries that happened in major accidents and on the battlefield. Many doctors employed procedures similar to those used by modern physicians. They knew how to sew up deep cuts with needle and thread, for instance, and applied wooden splints to help reset broken bones. They also performed various types of surgery.

These approaches to healing are listed in the *Book of Surgery*, today more often called the Edwin Smith Medical Papyrus (named after the American antiquities dealer who brought it to the attention of the archaeological world). Although it dates from the 1600s BCE, historians think many of the techniques it mentions were invented many centuries before. The excerpt that follows explains how to treat a person with a broken nose. "If you examine a man having a break of the column of his nose," it begins,

> his nose being disfigured, and a depression being in it, while the swelling that is on it protrudes, and he has discharged blood from both his nostrils; you should say concerning him, "One having a break of the column of his nose [is] an ailment which I will treat." You should clean it for him with two plugs of linen. You should place two other plugs of linen saturated with grease inside his two nostrils.[48]

The degree to which this and other examples of Egyptian healing were successful is unclear. What is more certain is that Egyptian doctors and the society they served devoted enormous time, energy, and resources to medical matters. This plainly shows that they sincerely desired to reduce human suffering, revealing a high level of caring and humanity that numerous other ancient cultures lacked. It is especially noteworthy that in the tomb of a twenty-fifth-century-BCE doctor named Nenkh-Sekhmet,

Looking Back

Women's Dresses in Art and Reality

In Egypt's first several centuries, the majority of women, rich and poor alike, wore a dress fashioned from a large piece of cloth that was gathered and sewn up along one side of the body. But depictions of such garments in art from the period are often misleading. Paintings frequently show these dresses clinging tightly to the body. However, actual surviving dresses from that era are looser, sometimes even baggy. Egyptologist Gay Robins explains why the artistic renderings did not match reality. In most ancient statues, he says,

> the dress hugs the body with no slack, so that the wearer appears to be hobbled. Most formal female figures have their feet almost together. When a figure needs to be shown in movement, the dress is extended just enough to allow this, as though it were elastic. Women are also portrayed sitting and kneeling in this garment, which still clings to the outline of the body. It is clear that the image is an artistic one and not one that could have existed in reality. Such an image ensures that the shape of the body is not obscured by the dress. Egyptian clothes were mostly made from linen, which tends to sag rather than cling. . . . By contrast, the sheath dress displays every curve of the body, including the stomach, buttocks, thighs, and breast, thus putting emphasis on the sexuality of the figure.

Gay Robins, *Women of Ancient Egypt*. Cambridge, MA: Harvard University Press, 1993, pp. 181–82.

excavators found an inscription that reads: "Never did I do anything evil towards any person."[49] These words sound strikingly similar to a phrase in the famous ancient Greek oath on which modern physicians' oaths are based. In it, a new doctor swore he would "never do harm to anyone."[50]

Informal Versus Formal Education

Another quality that set Egyptian doctors apart from average folk was that they were literate. In fact, they were among the country's small but highly influential group of individuals who had a formal education. A majority of Egyptians received what was essentially an informal education at the hands of their parents and sometimes other adult relatives. The age at which a child's education started differed according to the father's profession, the child's gender, and the family's social position.

In most lower-class families, for instance, mothers began teaching their daughters how to cook and make clothes when they were very young. Usually this was as far as their education went, and with occasional exceptions young women never attended school or learned to read and write. Girls from well-to-do families learned to sew, too, but were also instructed in singing, dancing, and playing musical instruments. Moreover, at least some young women from wealthy homes became literate, as evidenced by a few surviving letters that appear to have been written by women. As for boys from poorer homes, the majority learned an occupation or trade from their fathers or became apprentices to another tradesman.

In addition to practical or occupational skills, the informal education an average boy or girl received included basic social skills and a sense of morality. As Strouhal puts it, "Parents familiarized their children with their ideas about the world with their religious outlook, with their ethical principles, and with correct behavior toward others and toward the supernatural beings in whom everyone believed."[51]

By contrast, the fortunate few who received formal education had a very real leg up on everyone else. First, literacy gave them a shot at jobs in the national government, which carried with them high pay and social status. Beyond this handful of special workers, the majority of literate individuals became scribes—masters of reading and writing—who formed a small but very esteemed class within society's upper levels.

Indeed, scribes earned instant respect wherever they went, in large part because society could barely function without them. They penned diplomatic letters for rulers; kept official records for administrators, temples, merchants, and others; and acted as teachers to those who got a formal education. Considering the importance of scribes, upper-class parents often urged their sons to join their ranks, hoping, as Rosalie David says, those young men would be able to "escape the toil associated with all other trades."[52] Similarly, part of the advice a seasoned scribe offered young men aspiring to that vocation was to "set your mind to being a scribe, an excellent trade. You will walk unhindered on the road, and not become an ox to be handed over. You will be at the head of others."[53]

Exposure to Wisdom and Literature

When acting as teachers, scribes held classes in settings that ranged from the royal palace and religious temples to spare rooms in well-to-do homes that belonged to the parents of some of the students. The principal subjects taught were reading and writing. But a lot of time was also devoted to exposing the students to what modern scholars call "wisdom literature." This consisted of writings of various kinds and lengths that took the form of advice or instruction. A large number of them advocated the importance of honesty, hard work, justice, good manners, tolerance, and fair treatment of the poor and underprivileged.

By absorbing these concepts, David points out, the students increased their chances of "advancement in life" and of acquiring "the skills required in good leaders."[54] This aspect of formal education in Egypt may well have had momentous consequences for the country. Some historians have suggested that the strong emphasis teachers placed on honesty, justice, and fairness may have helped instill a positive moral outlook in many of the royal princes who eventually became pharaohs. This might explain why so many of them were unusually humane and constructive rulers. In turn, such leadership qualities may have inspired loyalty among the citizenry and thereby contributed to the tremendously long life that Egypt enjoyed as an independent nation.

Chapter Four

Workers, Occupations, and Crafts

Many modern books about ancient Egypt describe its people as hardworking and diligent, and no truer statement has ever been made. With the exception of a handful of privileged nobles and wealthy individuals, virtually every ancient Egyptian performed some sort of work on a daily basis. Moreover, most did so with a strong sense of personal responsibility to their fellow citizens. Many people today are hardworking, too, to be sure. But work in modern times is mainly viewed as a way to support oneself or one's family, rather than as essential to supporting and perpetuating the larger social system.

In contrast, the idea of shared responsibility and sacrifice was very relevant to the ancient Egyptians. Although most farmers were poor peasants and socially inferior to members of the upper classes, Egyptians placed high value on the work done by farmers. All available evidence, the late Egyptologist Adolf Erman wrote, "tends to show that the Egyptians themselves felt that agriculture was the most important industry in the country."[55] Conversely, the peasants and other members of the lower classes looked to the pharaoh, vizier, and other top officials to run the country and protect its citizenry. So overall there was a certain level of respect for the contributions made to the system by people of diverse social status and skill sets.

A Farmer's Life

The contributions made by farmers were indeed crucial to the life and survival of Egyptians. The farmers carefully followed traditional methods passed down from prior generations, an agricultural heritage almost unmatched in breadth and longevity in the ancient world. The first-century-BCE Greek historian Diodorus Siculus, who visited Egypt, commented that Egyptian farmers "have much more experience than the farmers among other peoples. They know the condition of the soil, the flow of the water, the correct time of sowing and reaping, and the further treatment of the harvest very precisely. This they learn partly from the observations of their forebears, and partly through their own perception."[56]

Using this accumulated knowledge, the farmers took full advantage of

Workers carry out a variety of jobs along the Nile River. The average person in ancient Egypt spent a lifetime working hard every day.

the country's unique geographical attributes. Well more than 90 percent of ancient Egypt was made up of dry, barren wastelands. Only in the lush green regions lying along the Nile's banks was it possible to grow enough food to sustain a large population. So if for one reason or another the

farmers did not live up to their responsibilities, mass starvation could be expected to bring the country down in short order.

To ensure that such a disaster did not occur, Egyptian farmers faithfully kept pace with the annual Nile floods, which provided the water necessary for large-scale irrigation. The slow-moving water carried the sediments that replenished the soil, rendering it incredibly fertile and ready for planting. Thus, "as soon as the waters began to recede," Egyptologist Fekri Hassan writes, "the farmers returned to their sodden fields to sow their seeds. The crops were ready for harvest from February to early June, when the Nile was at its lowest level."[57]

Planting and Harvest

To plant their wheat, lentils, cucumbers, onions, barley, leeks, flax, and other crops, the growers most often tossed out their seeds by hand from sacks slung over their necks or shoulders. They then worked the seeds into the soil using simple wooden plows drawn by cows, donkeys, or oxen. Some farmers did not bother to plow their land. Instead they turned loose their goats, pigs, sheep, and other farm animals, which trampled the seeds (*peret*) into the soil. Later, at harvest time, lines of workers walked through the fields swinging wooden sickles back and forth. Right behind them came teams of women and children, who scooped up the crops and loaded them into wicker baskets.

Between the end of the harvest and the conclusion of the yearly inundation, when it was time to begin planting again, most farmers had some free time either to rest or pursue other activities. It is possible that some made pottery and other crafts. But an undetermined number worked on government-sponsored tasks, especially big building projects like erecting palaces, temples, pyramids, and other large structures.

Such workers were often in high demand, as illustrated by a surviving decree issued by the pharaoh Seti I (reigned 1294–1279 BCE). He wanted to ensure that his temple at Abydos (in central Egypt) would be built on schedule. So he made it illegal for a contractor to conscript any of the workers who were laboring on that structure. The document warned that it was forbidden for "any troop-commander, or mayor, or agent, or any person" to try to use any workers at Abydos. Such a perpetrator was to be punished "by beating him with two hundred blows and five open wounds."[58]

Government Officials

On the opposite end of ancient Egypt's social and occupational spectrum was another job that was vital to the country—working for the government. Some of the leading government officials were nobles, priests, and other members of the upper classes, including scribes. A majority of scribes came from well-to-do families who could afford to educate them. Thus, most Egyptians who held cushy government positions did not start out poor and work their way up the professional and social ladder. In truth, there was little upward mobility in Egyptian society.

Exceptions to that rule are known, however. Among them was a man named Weni. He began in obscurity as a soldier in the army, and through talent and hard work he rose through the ranks. Eventually he served in official positions under three pharaohs of the late second millennium BCE—Teti, Pepi I, and Merenra. Finally, Weni was appointed governor of Upper Egypt. Historians know about the various important administrative jobs he held and the duties they entailed because he penned an autobiography that has survived. In one passage he brags about how King Merenra praised him for serving with distinction:

> I governed Upper Egypt for him in peace, so that no one attacked his fellow. I did every task. I counted everything that is countable for the residence in this Upper Egypt two times, and every service that is countable for the residence in this Upper Egypt two times. I did a perfect job in this Upper Egypt. Never before had the like been done in this Upper Egypt. I acted throughout so that his majesty praised me for it.[59]

Soldiers

Because Weni began as a soldier, he also offered valuable information about that profession, one of the largest and most important in Egypt. With some exceptions, most men entered the army's ranks by following in their fathers' footsteps. Military scribes carefully recorded the names of all soldiers on lists the government kept from one generation to the next. When a soldier retired or died in the line of duty, his son inherited his position, including any military benefits his father had earned.

Many young men entered the military because of a strong sense of family duty, therefore, as well as feelings of duty to country. Still, quite a few men became soldiers because they hoped to acquire booty, valuables collected on the job. Upon capturing an enemy camp or town, a pharaoh or military general seized as many horses, jewels, gold and silver objects, slaves, and other valuables as possible. It was expected that he would hand out a portion of this booty to his troops. Also, any prisoners a soldier captured on his own were his to keep or sell as he saw fit.

Still another benefit of soldiering was earning medals for bravery, which one could display with pride for the rest of one's life. In an autobiography, a soldier named Ahmose, who lived some eight centuries later than Weni, bragged about the medals he received, saying, "I showed valor on foot in the presence of his majesty."[60] Ahmose was awarded one of Egypt's highest honors, a medal called the Gold of Valor.

Regardless of the potential benefits, however, the life of a soldier, particularly when on a military campaign, could be both arduous and dangerous. There were long periods away from home and family; seemingly endless marches through barren, bleak territories; harsh discipline meted out by officers; large amounts of backbreaking labor; and exposure to all sorts of diseases—not to mention the risk of death on the battlefield.

Craftsmen and Artists

When a soldier managed to survive all of these dangers and threats and retired from the military, he commonly sought some other occupation that would provide a living for him and his family, if he had one. Some former soldiers took up farming. Many others became craftsmen—highly

In Their Own Words

Do Not Become a Soldier!

A large number of documents written by Egyptian scribes have survived. Among them are some satirical, or tongue-in-cheek, warnings to students to stay away from most or all occupations that feature menial or hard work. In this example a scribe singles out and mocks the professional soldier, whose life supposedly consists of one arduous or painful duty after another. He is forced to wake up at all hours of the night, the scribe claims, and he must toil even after "the sun sets in the darkness of night." The scribe continues:

> He is hungry. His belly hurts. He is dead while yet alive. When he receives the grain ration, having been released from duty, it is not good for grinding. He is called up to [march to] Syria. He may not rest. There are no clothes, no sandals. [On the way to Syria] his march is uphill through mountains. He drinks water every third day. It is smelly and tastes of salt. His body is ravaged by illness. The enemy comes, surrounds him with missiles [spears and arrows] and life recedes from him. He is told, "Quick, forward valiant soldier! Win for yourself a good name!" [But] he does not know what he is about. His body is weak. His legs fail him. When victory is won . . . his wife and children are in their village. He dies and does not reach it. If he comes out alive, he is worn out from marching.

Quoted in Miriam Lichtheim, *Ancient Egyptian Literature: A Book of Readings*, vol. 2. Berkeley: University of California Press, 1976, p. 172.

skilled workers, most of whom had not started out as soldiers. Numerous different kinds of craftsmen— mostly men but a fair number of women, too—existed in Egypt. Only a partial list includes potters; carpenters; coppersmiths; smiths who specialized in other metals, including bronze, gold, and silver; jewelers; leather workers; basket makers; glassmakers; tailors and seamstresses; and stonemasons.

Joining the ranks of these craft specialists were professional workers of a different sort—men and women who today are classified as artists. For reasons that are unclear, the Egyptians did not have a separate word for *artist* in the modern sense. Rather, the upper classes viewed talented individuals like painters, sculptors, and musicians simply as other kinds of craft specialists and granted them the same social status and pay as craftsmen.

Among these talented persons who were not accorded the title of artist were numerous women. It has been established that Egyptian women served in many occupations both inside and outside household settings, including cooks, maids, weavers, bakers, and even a few doctors. More artistically talented women worked either part- or full-time as flower arrangers, beauticians, musicians, dancers, singers, painters, and possibly as assistants to jewelers and sculptors.

WORDS IN CONTEXT
kedu
Potters, who fashioned both cheap articles made from mud and finer ones made from stone dust.

Whether female or male, most craftsmen were not independent contractors who worked for themselves, as their modern counterparts often are. Instead, they usually did their jobs in workshops, the ancient equivalent of factories, owned by the royal palace, temples, provincial governors, and wealthy households. The main reason for this was that a majority of the craftsmen's customers were members of the upper classes. The peasants who made up the bulk of the population usually could not afford to buy the finely made products created by the craftsmen and artists. André Dollinger offers two examples, saying, "Cabinet makers carefully carved beautiful furniture for the rich, while the less well-off made do with often crudely made and painted chests and chairs, and the poor had to do without. Seamstresses sewed dresses of the finest linen, while the peasant woman's handiwork was much simpler and cheaper."[61]

Potters

One of the few exceptions to this rule consisted of cheap dinnerware and vases made by *kedu*, or potters, who were probably the earliest Egyptian craft specialists, as well as the most common. The diverse kinds of pottery, or ceramic items, they produced included dishes, cups, bowls, jugs, oil flasks, flower vases, wine jars, oil-burning lamps, and figurines, to name only a few. Modern scholars refer to most of

Using a saw and other implements, workers keep busy in an ancient Egyptian carpentry workshop. Other craftsmen of the era included potters, metalsmiths, glassmakers, seamstresses, and stonemasons.

these objects as coarse ware. They were made from mud from the riverbanks, intended for practical purposes, and inexpensive. So all but the very poorest families could afford to purchase at least a few of them. A smaller number of ceramic items were fashioned of faience, which was composed of stone dust rather than mud. Faience wares were much higher in quality, more expensive, and more often than not marketed to the upper classes.

In Egypt's earliest centuries, potters created coarse ware totally by hand. Sometime between 3000 and 2400 BCE, however, the first potter's wheel came into use in Egypt. Whether it was invented there or imported from Mesopotamia or elsewhere is a point still debated by historians. In the earliest version, the potter turned the wheel with his left hand while molding the pot with his right, which made it hard to make a jar or some other item symmetrical and well proportioned. An improved wheel appeared in the mid-1000s BCE. It allowed an assistant to spin the wheel while the potter shaped the object with both hands. Increasingly better wheels came into use in the centuries that followed, most notably the pedal-operated kick wheel introduced into Egypt by the Greeks in the late first millennium BCE.

The fact that so much of their merchandise was common and cheap negatively affected the reputation of many potters. Indeed, they were among the least esteemed of Egyptian craftsmen. In a document dating to about 1950 BCE, a scribe urges his son to avoid the potter's profession because the work is often messy and lowly. A potter's clothes are "stiff with slime," the father says, "and his leather apron is in tatters." Furthermore, "the air which enters up his nose spews directly from his kiln."[62]

Smiths and Jewelers

Smiths of various types also worked under gritty, at times even foul, conditions. Smoke from their furnaces, along with their constant sweating and the odors given off by the smelted metals, seems to have made their workshops stink badly. A passage written by a person who had visited a coppersmith's shop cautioned, "He stinks more than fish eggs!"[63] Making matters worse, the writer said, the heat these workers endured day in and day out made the skin on their hands look like a crocodile's hide.

An Egyptian smith's working conditions aside, his job was crucial to the country. The copper, bronze, and iron he produced were used for making spear tips, swords, and other weapons, without which the army would have been defenseless against invaders. Also, the gold and silver the smith extracted from ores were major assets of the nation's royalty and upper classes, as well as key ingredients of one of society's most coveted and treasured commodities—jewelry.

Egyptian jewelers made both cheap costume jewelry for members of the lower classes and expensive items for the well-to-do. Among the latter were some of the finest necklaces, bracelets, earrings, anklets, and pendants of the ancient world. The necklaces included both simple, single strands and a much wider and more elaborate variety called *wesekh*. Even more complex was the pectoral. It could be either a necklace with an ornately decorated plaque hanging from it or the plaque itself, which was frequently worn like a brooch. The plaque usually contained a detailed painted or carved miniature scene containing beautiful pieces of stone, metal, and other materials. In addition to gold and silver, jewelers employed copper; bronze; electrum (a mixture of gold and silver); brass (a mixture of copper and zinc); ivory; polished colored pebbles; glass beads; seashells; and semiprecious stones that included garnet, lapis lazuli, turquoise, carnelian, jasper, rock crystal, calcite, feldspar, and quartz, among others.

> **WORDS IN CONTEXT**
> *wesekh*
> Wide, elaborate necklaces worn by both women and men.

Fine Egyptian jewelry was not only worn by both female and male members of the upper classes, it was also used to decorate statues of the gods that stood inside temples. In addition, wealthy folk adorned the bodies of their deceased loved ones with various jewelry items before sealing their tombs. A virtual treasure trove of more than two hundred magnificent jewelry items was found in 1922 in the tomb of the boy-pharaoh Tutankhamun (better known today as "King Tut"), who reigned around 1336 to 1327 BCE. Of these objects, among the more stunning are a bracelet decorated with a pure gold scarab beetle inlaid with blue

Looking Back

A Painting Brings Planting to Life

Many of the paintings found in Egyptian tombs depict workers of various kinds in the midst of doing their jobs. This excerpt from a book by the late British Museum scholar T.G.H. James describes a series of paintings showing a farmer and five helpers plowing and planting seeds. James also provides a vivid description of an ancient Egyptian plow.

> Two pairs [of men] drag forward the plow, which is controlled by an elderly man, his age and somewhat superior status indicated by his thin, wispy hair and his paunch [pot belly]. A young man completes the group. He walks behind the plow, casting seed into the furrow. The plow is very simple, consisting of a pole, at the lower end of which a wooden share [blade] is loosely attached, and prevented from forming too wide an angle with the share by a twisted rope. From the same end of the pole rises the handle, used more to hold the share down in the furrow than to control the direction. The old man clearly presses down as they move forward. The design of this typical Egyptian plow is primitive, but very effective. . . . It is rather unusual to have a plow drawn by manpower, a task usually performed by cattle. [Yet] the laborers appointed to do this work do not appear to be too dispirited.

T.G.H. James, *Pharaoh's People: Scenes from Life in Imperial Egypt.* London: Tauris Parke, 2003, p. 107.

pieces of lapis lazuli, and a necklace with an attached falcon pendant containing turquoise, carnelian, lapis lazuli, and gold. These and many other surviving examples of ancient Egyptian jewelry have inspired countless outpourings of praise by modern experts. Typical is that of the late noted English art historian Cyril Aldred. "The superb skill and taste of the Egyptian goldsmith," he stated, "have never been surpassed."[64]

Sculptors

Fine jewelry settings like those made for royalty were only one of several examples of superb artistry among Egyptian craftsmen. Among the others was the work of the country's sculptors, who produced both freestanding statues and bas-reliefs (carved figures and scenes raised from but still attached to a flat surface). The reliefs were most often carved on large horizontal stone panels in temples, tombs, and palaces.

These renderings followed a number of artistic conventions, or rules of style, that gave them a somewhat stiff, unnatural look. About these conventions, Lionel Casson wrote:

A pharaoh is rendered as a giant among pygmies. He is shown with his head and legs in profile, but with his chest, shoulders, and one eye turned toward the viewer. A herd of cattle is shown in a formal line so there could be no mistaking its number or condition, rather than as a confused mass of heads and bodies and legs, as it would appear in life. Such conventions, and not the wish to capture nature, are the language of Egyptian artists.[65]

The freestanding statues the sculptors created were carved from several different materials, including stone, metal, wood, terra-cotta (baked clay), and ivory. The figures pictured gods, pharaohs and their wives and children, government officials, various other people, and a wide variety of animals. Although most statues were life-size or a bit smaller or larger than life-size, a few were enormous. Among the most renowned of these so-called colossi are two stone images of the pharaoh Amenhotep III (reigned ca. 1390–1352 BCE). Each stands some 50 feet (15 m) high and weighs more than 700 tons (635 metric tons). The largest of all the statues produced in ancient Egypt is the famous Great Sphinx at Giza (near modern Cairo), measuring roughly 66 feet (20 m) high and 240 feet (73 m) long.

Painters

Like sculptors, painters captured the essence of their subjects while employing traditional artistic conventions. These rules included some of the same ones followed in reliefs and statues. They might show the head in profile with one eye visible, for instance, or twist the torso completely to the front, making the body "appear distorted and internally inconsistent to modern eyes,"[66] in Ian Shaw's words.

Another convention Egyptian painters used was arranging their individual illustrations into horizontal bands called registers. Often a painted wall displayed several of these bands, each located above or below another. The registers were meant to tell a story in chronological order, so that the events depicted in the lowest register were the most recent and the higher ones took the viewer increasingly far into the past.

The paintings were both large and small and adorned the surfaces of all manner of objects, materials, and settings. They included statues and figurines; wooden chests and other storage boxes, coffins, funerary masks, linen that had been stiffened with plaster, paper made from the papyrus plant, pillars, and most common of all—walls.

When creating a painting that covered an entire wall, painters worked in groups of two, three, or more. This is described in a surviving letter written by a painter named Hor-Min to his father, a scribe. Hor-Min mentions that he had been working alongside his brother, also a painter, to decorate the walls of a large tomb. Hor-Min requests that his father, who apparently supervised a number of artists, send someone to "give me a hand with the painting. I am alone, since my brother is ill."[67]

No one knows which tomb painting Hor-Min was working on at

the time and whether it has survived. What is certain is that, like the vast majority of Egyptian workers in a wide range of occupations, he took pride in his job and was extremely concerned with doing it to the best of his ability. Unlike most other workers, he labored in a very distinctive profession. He and his fellow artists crafted a vivid, lasting record of Egyptian life, making it possible for hundreds of future generations to know and marvel at their fascinating civilization.

Chapter Five

Religious Beliefs and Rituals

Herodotus's famous remark that the Egyptians were the most religiously devout people in the world has repeatedly been confirmed by modern experts. Rosalie David sums up the main thrust of the combined archaeological, literary, and artistic evidence, saying, "Religion was an integral part of the lives of the ancient Egyptians and permeated most aspects of everyday existence, in addition to laying the foundation for their funerary beliefs and customs."[68]

Roots of the Religion

One crucial fact that remains uncertain is how Egyptian religion originally developed. What historians do know is that at first, people worshipped diverse gods on the local level. Before Egypt became a unified nation, its inhabitants dwelled in separate, often somewhat culturally distinct regions, each of which had its own creator god, deity of the dead, war god, and so forth.

Apparently, the early Egyptians viewed these deities as somewhat human-like versions of the natural forces they observed all around them. To ensure that those forces would affect humanity in benign, positive ways, it seemed only logical that people should appease them with various forms of worship. Researcher Jill Kamil explains:

> The regularity of nature's forces provided the basis for the ancient
> Egyptians' sense of order and balance. Like many other early so-
> cieties, their religious focus was on nature, which provided their
> means of existence. They were able to explain the origins of life in

relation to their environment. Their early observations of nature and the solar forces were later incorporated into the doctrine that formed the basis of the official religion.[69]

Each of the local regions that existed before pharaonic times developed its personalized version of divine creation and viewed its own favorite gods as the agents of that creation. Later, when Narmer brought those disunited districts together into a single nation, he recognized how important the local gods, myths, and religious customs of those regions were to their residents. He sought to join those numerous scattered gods, beliefs, myths, and rituals together into a single religious structure.

But the first pharaoh shrewdly realized that if he wanted to earn everyone's trust and allegiance, he could not deprive some of his subjects of their traditional and beloved religious beliefs and customs. So he employed an inclusive rather than exclusive strategy. His new national religion was nothing less than an overflowing melting pot of divine beings and religious beliefs and rituals. This explains why Egypt had so many gods and separate beliefs and myths, some of which overlapped in function and even sometimes contradicted one another.

> **WORDS IN CONTEXT**
> **cosmogonies**
> Creation stories of a people or religion.

Stories of Creation

A clear example of such overlap and contradiction was the array of cosmogonies, or creation myths, the Egyptians came to believe in. Atum, Ptah, Amun, and other deities were all seen as creator gods in separate stories that each envisioned the emergence of the world and humans in a somewhat different way. Atum, for example, supposedly fashioned the *ben-ben*, a sacred mound that was the first land in a limitless sea, using his hands, as a potter would shape a bowl. In contrast, the creation myth involving Ptah envisioned him bringing the various elements of the universe into being using merely the power of his voice. Another distinction among the creation tales was that the initial groups of deities crafted by each creator god were different.

A nobleman and his wife make offerings of food to the Egyptian fertility god Osiris. Egyptians also believed that Osiris was responsible for the annual flooding of the Nile, an event that was essential both for prosperity and survival.

Despite such inconsistencies, the Egyptians viewed all these myths as equally acceptable, because to them they were not strictly factual accounts. Instead, the cosmogonies were thought to be filled with symbolism and mystery—elements the human mind was not meant to understand. Hence, it was assumed that all the creation tales had some spark of truth.

Gods of Nature and Life

Beside creator gods like Ptah and Atum, the Egyptians recognized several major deities, each of which oversaw some aspect of nature and life. Especially important was Ra (or Re), the sun god, who was thought to traverse the sky during the daytime and travel beneath the earth, in a region called the Duat, at night. Somewhere in the Duat existed the Underworld, the realm of the dead, overseen by the mighty fertility god Osiris. People believed that Osiris also set in motion the Nile's inundation each year, bringing humanity the means of survival and prosperity.

No less important to the Egyptians was Osiris's sister and wife, Isis, also a fertility deity. It was believed that she ensured there would be regular harvests of wheat and the other grains vital to the country's continued success. In addition, Isis was seen as a loving mother figure. In art she was commonly viewed cradling her young son, Horus.

A physical depiction of Isis as her worshippers believed she appeared survives in *The Golden Ass*, a novel by the Roman writer Apuleius. "Her lofty head was encircled by a garland interwoven with diverse blossoms," it says in part. "She wore a multicolored dress woven from fine linen, one part of which shone radiantly white, a second glowed yellow with saffron blossom, and a third blazed rosy red."[70]

In addition to these and a few other major gods, the Egyptians worshipped a host of minor divinities. Only a brief list includes Hathor, goddess of beauty and love, who often took the form of a cow; the falcon-headed Montu, one of several war gods; Sobek, who ensured the growth of water plants; Kherty, protector of tombs; Taweret, who watched over women during childbirth; Thoth, deity of learning and wisdom; and Anubis, god of the dead.

The Myth of Kingship

Along with this great pantheon, or group of gods worshipped by society, the early Egyptians held that their pharaoh had a divine spark. (Historians think this belief faded over time, until in Egypt's final centuries it was more a superstition accepted by a few but rejected by the majority.) This idea came from one of the most important and revered of the country's religious tales, today called the Myth of Kingship.

In the story the grownup Horus fought and defeated his uncle—Osiris's and Isis's brother Seth (or Set). Horus then took the throne as Egypt's first pharaoh. More significantly, thereafter each pharaoh carried part of Horus's spirit, so that he *was* the divine Horus as long as he lived and ruled. After a pharaoh died, however, he became one with Horus's father, Osiris, ruler of the kingdom of the dead.

Belief in the Myth of Kingship strongly affected religious rituals and customs in Egypt. "Each king," says Ian Shaw, came to be seen "as a combination of the divine and the mortal in the same way that the living king was linked with Horus, and the dead kings, the royal ancestors, were associated with Horus's father Osiris."[71] Therefore, the living pharaoh received worship, including offerings of prayer and gifts, and so did past pharaohs. Special temples were erected for them in which priests conducted rituals intended to make sure those rulers prospered in the afterlife. In addition, sacred paintings showed aspects of the famous battle between Horus and Seth, often depicting the two as hippos thrashing in the river. Also, each year a magnificent religious mystery play was presented at Edfu, in central Egypt. Actors in colorful costumes portrayed the battling Horus and Seth, and after the performance worshippers feasted to celebrate Horus's victory.

> **WORDS IN CONTEXT**
> *ben-ben*
> In Egyptian mythology, the sacred mound making up the first piece of land to appear on earth.

The Importance of Rituals

Worshipping both living and deceased kings and commemorating sacred stories in art and onstage were only a few of the religious rituals of the ancient Egyptians. In fact, rituals lay at the heart of their religious life. Most modern faiths, including Judaism, Christianity, and Islam, have time-honored rituals, too, such as going to a synagogue, church, or mosque and reciting passages from holy books. Yet it is belief in God that is the central pillar of these religions. Even someone who fails to perform the rituals can claim to be an adherent as long as he or she believes.

The ancient Egyptians saw the situation very differently, however. To them, believing in the gods was a given, as no one questioned their existence. Also, they had no special holy writings like the Torah, New Testament, or Koran, nor did they venerate any divinely inspired list

In Their Own Words

The Negative Confession

The Egyptians believed that upon reaching Osiris's kingdom, a recently deceased person came before that god and a panel of other divine judges. If those beings felt the person had led a decent life, he or she made it into the afterlife. To help guide the judges' decision, society developed a group of phrases and speeches that a person could memorize in life and then after death recite to Osiris and his scary colleagues. These words, which insisted the person had never committed any serious sins, are today often called the "negative confession." It says in part:

> I have acted rightly in Egypt. I have not cursed a god. I have not been faulted. Hail to you, gods in the Hall of the Two Truths, who have no lies in their bodies, who live on *maat* [order or justice] in On [the holy city of Heliopolis], who feed on the rightness before Horus in his disk. Rescue me from Babi [a bloodthirsty baboon-headed god], who feeds on the entrails of nobles on that day of the great reckoning. Behold me, I have come to you without sin, without guilt, without evil, without a witness against me, without one whom I have wronged. I live on *maat*, feed on *maat*. I have done what people speak of, what the gods are pleased with. I have contented a god with what he wishes. I have given bread to the hungry, water to the thirsty!

Quoted in Miriam Lichtheim, *Ancient Egyptian Literature: A Book of Readings*, vol. 2. Berkeley: University of California Press, 1976, p. 128.

of religious principles. The Egyptians expressed their faith almost completely through their actions—namely, rituals that honored, appeased, or sought to communicate with the gods.

The main reason for performing the rituals was to guarantee "the continuation of existence itself,"[72] as scholar Richard H. Wilkinson puts it. People believed the gods were not only capable of destroying the world, but might actually do so at any moment if provoked by bad human behavior. The world and humanity would continue to go on, Wilkinson explains, only if people kept up regular "practice of rituals which supported the gods so that they in turn might be able to preserve and sustain the world."[73]

Ritual Sacrifices

Of the many rituals, the most widespread and important consisted of offerings, or sacrifices, to the gods. These could take the form of liquids such as milk, honey, or wine, which were set before or poured over an altar stone. Flowers and other kinds of plants were also offered.

More common, however, were animal sacrifices. Cows, goats, sheep, or other creatures were slaughtered and parts of them burned on an altar. It was thought that the smoke from the burning beast rose up into the sky and provided one or more gods with welcome nourishment. This ceremony and the theory behind it were repeated century after century not only in Egypt but in lands across the ancient world.

Herodotus had witnessed such rituals in his native land, and after visiting Egypt he made sure to describe the local version in his book so that his Greek readers could compare it with their own practices. Egyptians who desired to perform a sacrifice, he wrote, would take an animal "to an appropriate altar and light a fire." Then, after pouring a liquid offering of wine on the altar, they butchered the creature, sliced off its head, and cut up the carcass. Having finished slaughtering the animal, he continued, they first pray, and then take its belly out whole, leaving the intestines and fat inside the body. Next they cut off the legs, shoulder, neck, and rump, and stuff the carcass with loaves of bread, honey, raisins, figs, frankincense, myrrh, and other nice-smelling substances. Finally, they pour a quantity of oil over the body and burn it. They always fast before a sacrifice, and while the fire is consuming it, they beat their breasts.[74]

Another type of sacrificial gift to the gods—known as a votive offering—was not meant to feed or pacify a deity. Instead, someone made a votive offering either in exchange for a god doing that person a favor or to thank the divinity for answering a prayer. Such offerings sometimes consisted of flowers, food, and/or beverages. Other common votive gifts included wooden, metal, or pottery statuettes of deities or pharaohs. People placed votive offerings on altars or in other spots where it was thought the gods might notice them. It was also accepted practice to carve or paint a request for a divine favor onto a wooden or stone slab called a stele. In the mid-second millennium BCE, worshippers started drawing or carving human ears onto stelae based on the notion that this would help a god hear the message.

The Roles of Priests

Any person in ancient Egypt was qualified to perform a sacrifice or make a votive offering. Yet when priests carried out a sacrifice it had weightier significance, since these individuals worked in temples and had access to the holiest chambers and statues of the gods. Egyptian priests performed several other important religious rituals as well.

These priests were very different from ministers, rabbis, imams, and other modern clergy. An Egyptian priest was a servant of a god, or the gods in general, whose main job was to execute the traditional rituals associated with the divine beings. As David points out, priests did not get involved with the spiritual or personal needs of everyday people. The priests "had no pastoral duties," she says, "and were not expected to preach to the people or oversee their moral welfare. Indeed, they played

Egyptian priests lead worshippers in a ritual honoring a deity in the form of a bull. The primary duty of the priests was not ministering to the needs of the people but rather performing the rituals that celebrated and served the gods.

no direct role in developing the religious awareness or beliefs of the masses."[75] Rather, the priests were simply devoted religious officials who were trained to carry out their duties efficiently.

Besides sacrifice, the key ritual the priests performed was to tend to the blessed images of gods that rested inside the temples. Typical duties included washing the sacred statues; moving them outside the temples during certain religious festivals; and overseeing the craftsmen who decorated the temples and the servants who cleaned them. While doing their daily tasks, the priests followed strict rules, several of them related to cleanliness. Herodotus reported that they shaved their bodies on a regular basis and that they "wear linen only, and shoes made from the papyrus plant. These materials, for dress and shoes, [are] the only ones allowed them. They bathe in cold water twice a day and twice every night, and observe innumerable other ceremonies besides."[76]

Festivals and Divine Communication

The religious festivals during which priests carried some of the divine statues outside the temples were activities that all Egyptians looked forward to. The largest ones took place on national holidays. Of these, one of the most popular was the New Year Festival, celebrated on July 19—the day that the brightest star in the night sky, Sirius, appeared above a set point on the horizon.

Even bigger was the Festival of Opet, held in the second month of the Nile's inundation. Lasting from two to four weeks, it attracted huge crowds of worshippers decked out in their finest outfits. They watched the priests of the sprawling temple complex at Karnak (near Thebes) carry a group of sacred statues along a road lined by stone sphinxes to another temple. In addition to this ceremony, people throughout the country prayed, sacrificed, danced, and feasted.

During the Opet event and other religious festivals, as well as at other times of the year, worshippers attempted to communicate with the gods. Prayer was the most common way. Usually a person addressed the god by name, heaped praises on that being, and then requested something, such as recovery from an illness, a good harvest, or victory in a battle or war.

People also communicated with the divine through oracles. These were statues or people thought to be able to convey messages back and forth between humans and gods. In addition, the Egyptians believed they could contact a god during a dream. In a procedure called incubation, a deity supposedly paid a sleeping person a visit and in some cases described one or more future events.

> **WORDS IN CONTEXT**
> **incubation**
> In Egypt and some other ancient societies, a god's supposed visit to a person during the latter's dream.

Never to Be Extinguished

One future event that all Egyptians hoped to experience was reaching the afterlife, where they might live on for eternity. "No civilization ever devoted so much of its energies and resources to the quest for immortality

Looking Back

Preserving the Cosmic Order

University of Chicago scholar Emily Teeter here neatly explains some of the reasons why traditional and repeated rituals were, together, the prime moving force within ancient Egyptian religion.

> In the Egyptian mind, mortals should seek to ensure, through their rituals, the continuation of cosmic order and the benevolence of the gods and goddesses who controlled the universe. Egyptian rituals were primarily concerned with maintaining the image of a deity and offering it food and sustenance. The idea that an act of worship could propitiate [appease] a god is reflected in the fact that the Egyptian word for "offering," *hetep*, is the same as "to be at peace." Because rituals are repetitive, each one echoes all those that have gone before. Ritual gave structure to the past, which the Egyptians viewed with profound reverence. The state of the world was considered to have been perfect at its creation. Change was not necessarily viewed as progress, but more likely as an undesirable deviation. As unchanging re-enactments of ancient events, actions, and utterances, rituals contributed to the preservation of the ideal condition of the universe.

Emily Teeter, "The Life of Ritual," in *Ancient Egypt*, ed. David P. Silverman. New York: Oxford University Press, 2003, p. 148.

as did Egypt's,"[77] comments historian Bob Brier. One did not automatically make it to the afterlife. Instead, it was believed that a person had to behave ethically in his or her life on earth, so many people became preoccupied with avoiding sin. Another widely common concern was making proper preparations for death, including preserving the body after death. When possible, bodies were mummified, or embalmed using natron, a mineral salt that sucked most moisture from the corpse. The body was wrapped in strips of cloth before burial.

However, even assuming these conditions were met and the person's soul made it to Osiris's subterranean kingdom, the Egyptians did not expect that paradise awaited. Rather, they believed one's earthly life more or less continued in the afterlife. Thus, a potter remained a potter and performed the same activities in the next life as he had in the first.

Yet at least people would still be alive and conscious, an Egyptian reasoned. They would not have to face the horror of extinction and the jarring end of feelings and awareness. Also, if they, their family, and their neighbors achieved everlasting survival, their beloved nation might also endure, never to be extinguished. Indeed, the ancient Egyptians' strivings to ensure life beyond death "made the civilization immortal," Lionel Casson observed. "And in its zeal for conservation, it left to posterity the remains of a memorable grandeur."[78]

Source Notes

Introduction: People of Extraordinary Devotion

1. Herodotus, *The Histories*, trans. Aubrey de Sélincourt. New York: Penguin, 1978, p. 142.
2. Herodotus, *The Histories*, p. 143.
3. Lionel Casson, *Ancient Egypt*. New York: Time-Life Books, 1983, p. 71.
4. Casson, *Ancient Egypt*, p. 77.
5. Rosalie David, *Handbook to Life in Ancient Egypt*. New York: Oxford University Press, 2007, p. 281.

Chapter One: Houses and Home Life

6. May Mohamed, "The Palaces of Ancient Egypt," *Ancient Egypt* (blog), 2011. http://monumentsinegypt.blogspot.com.
7. Mohamed, "The Palaces of Ancient Egypt."
8. James F. Romano, *Daily Life of the Ancient Egyptians*. Pittsburgh, PA: Carnegie Museum of Natural History, 1990, p. 24.
9. Romano, *Daily Life of the Ancient Egyptians*, p. 25.
10. Eugen Strouhal, *Life of the Ancient Egyptians*. Norman: University of Oklahoma Press, 1992, p. 86.
11. Herodotus, *The Histories*, pp. 142–43.
12. Strouhal, *Life of the Ancient Egyptians*, p. 86.
13. Quoted in Strouhal, *Life of the Ancient Egyptians*, p. 87.
14. T.G.H. James, *Pharaoh's People: Scenes from Life in Imperial Egypt*. New York: Tauris Parke, 2003, p. 235.
15. James, *Pharaoh's People*, p. 235.
16. Strouhal, *Life of the Ancient Egyptians*, p. 103.
17. André Dollinger, "Pharaonic Egypt: Furniture," Ancient Egypt, May 2000. http://www.reshafim.org.
18. Herodotus, *The Histories*, p. 153.
19. Romano, *Daily Life of the Ancient Egyptians*, p. 35.
20. Herodotus, *The Histories*, p. 158.

21. "Proverbs of Ptah-hotep," in *Never to Die: The Egyptians in Their Own Words*, ed. Josephine Mayer and Tom Prideaux. New York: Viking, 1961, p. 53.

22. Herodotus, *The Histories*, pp. 158–59.

23. Romano, *Daily Life of the Ancient Egyptians*, p. 35.

Chapter Two: Social Relationships and Duties

24. Casson, *Ancient Egypt*, p. 52.

25. David, *Handbook to Life in Ancient Egypt*, p. 91.

26. Quoted in S.R.K. Glanville, *Catalogue of Demotic Papyri in the British Museum*, vol. 1. London: British Museum Press, 1955, pp. 20–21.

27. Quoted in Strouhal, *Life of the Ancient Egyptians*, p. 59.

28. Strouhal, *Life of the Ancient Egyptians*, p. 59.

29. Quoted in André Dollinger, "Pharaonic Egypt: Love Songs," Ancient Egypt, February 2004. www.reshafim.org.

30. Quoted in John L. Foster, trans., *Ancient Egyptian Literature*. Austin: University of Texas Press, 2001, p. 90.

31. May Mohamed, "Marriage and Divorce in Ancient Egypt," *Ancient Egypt* (blog), 2011. http://monumentsinegypt.blogspot.com.

32. Quoted in Janet H. Johnson and Edward F. Wente, eds., *Studies in Honor of George R. Hughes*. Chicago: Oriental Institute, 1976, p. 270.

33. Quoted in A.G. McDowell, *Village Life in Ancient Egypt*. New York: Oxford University Press, 1999, p. 47.

34. Quoted in McDowell, *Village Life in Ancient Egypt*, p. 35.

35. Strabo, *Geography*, vol. 4, trans. Horace L. Jones. Cambridge, MA: Harvard University Press, 1927, p. 153.

36. David, *Handbook to Life in Ancient Egypt*, p. 322.

37. Quoted in Miriam Lichtheim, *Ancient Egyptian Literature: A Book of Readings*, vol. 2. Berkeley: University of California Press, 1976, p. 188.

38. Quoted in Lichtheim, *Ancient Egyptian Literature: A Book of Readings*, vol. 1. Berkeley: University of California Press, 1973, p. 55.

Chapter Three: Personal Care, Health, and Education

39. Quoted in James H. Breasted, *Ancient Records of Egypt*, vol. 2. Chicago: University of Chicago Press, 2001, p. 196.

40. André Dollinger, "Pharaonic Egypt: Personal Hygiene and Cosmetics," Ancient Egypt, April 2013. www.reshafim.org.

41. Herodotus, *The Histories*, p. 143.

42. May Mohamed, "Ancient Egyptian Clothes," *Ancient Egypt* (blog), 2011. http://monumentsinegypt.blogspot.com.

43. Herodotus, *The Histories*, p. 134.

44. Strouhal, *Life of the Ancient Egyptians*, p. 74.

45. Strouhal, *Life of the Ancient Egyptians*, p. 74.

46. Quoted in Mayer and Prideaux, *Never to Die*, p. 77.

47. Quoted in André Dollinger, "Pharaonic Egypt: Extracts from the Ebers Medical Papyrus," Ancient Egypt, May 2003. www.reshafim.org.

48. Quoted in Logan Clendening, ed., *Source Book of Medical History*. New York: Dover, 1960, p. 2.

49. Quoted in Sameh M. Arab, "Medicine in Ancient Egypt, Part 3," Arab World Books. www.arabworldbooks.com.

50. Quoted in Association of American Physicians and Surgeons, "Physician Oaths." www.aapsonline.org/ethics/oaths.htm.

51. Strouhal, *Life of the Ancient Egyptians*, p. 31.

52. David, *Handbook to Life in Ancient Egypt*, p. 204.

53. Quoted in James, *Pharaoh's People*, p. 143.

54. David, *Handbook to Life in Ancient Egypt*, p. 207.

Chapter Four: Workers, Occupations, and Crafts

55. Adolf Erman, *Life in Ancient Egypt*, trans. H.M. Tirard. Charleston, SC: Nabu, 2010, p. 445.

56. Diodorus Siculus, *Library of History*, vol. 1, trans. C. Bradford Welles. Cambridge, MA: Harvard University Press, 1963, p. 255.

57. Fekri Hassan, "The Gift of the Nile," in *Ancient Egypt*, ed. David P. Silverman. New York: Oxford University Press, 1997, pp. 11–12.

58. Quoted in Kenneth A. Kitchen, *Ramesside Inscriptions*, vol. 2. New York: Oxford University Press, 1975, pp. 46–47.

59. Quoted in Lichtheim, *Ancient Egyptian Literature*, vol. 1, p. 21.

60. Quoted in James B. Pritchard, ed., *Ancient Near Eastern Texts Relating to the Old Testament*. Princeton, NJ: Princeton University Press, 1969, p. 233.

61. André Dollinger, "Pharaonic Egypt: Craftsmen and Artists," Ancient Egypt, June 2009. http://www.reshafim.org.

62. Quoted in Foster, *Ancient Egyptian Literature*, p. 35.

63. Quoted in James, *Pharaoh's People*, p. 181.

64. Cyril Aldred, *Middle Kingdom Art in Ancient Egypt, 2300–1590 B.C.* London: Alec Tiranti, 1950, p. 26.

65. Casson, *Ancient Egypt*, p. 124.

66. Ian Shaw, "Art," in *The Dictionary of Ancient Egypt*, by Ian Shaw and Paul Nicholson. New York: Abrams, 1995, p. 39.

67. Quoted in McDowell, *Village Life in Ancient Egypt*, p. 215.

Chapter Five: Religious Beliefs and Rituals

68. David, *Handbook to Life in Ancient Egypt*, p. 101.

69. Jill Kamil, *The Ancient Egyptians: Life in the Old Kingdom*. Cairo: American University in Cairo Press, 1996, p. 34.

70. Apuleius, *The Golden Ass*, trans. P.G. Walsh. New York: Oxford University Press, 1995, pp. 219–20.

71. Ian Shaw, ed., *The Oxford History of Ancient Egypt*. New York: Oxford University Press, 2000, p. 9.

72. Richard H. Wilkinson, *The Complete Gods and Goddesses of Ancient Egypt*. London: Thames and Hudson, 2003, p. 43.

73. Wilkinson, *The Complete Gods and Goddesses of Ancient Egypt*, p. 43.

74. Herodotus, *The Histories*, pp. 144–45.

75. David, *Handbook to Life in Ancient Egypt*, p. 109.

76. Herodotus, *The Histories*, p. 143.

77. Bob Brier, "Egyptomania: What Accounts for Our Intoxication with Things Egyptian?," *Archaeology*, January–February 2004, p. 18.

78. Casson, *Ancient Egypt*, p. 80.

For Further Research

Books

Crispin Boyer, *National Geographic Kids: Everything Ancient Egypt*. Des Moines, IA: National Geographic, 2012.

Bob Brier and Hoyt Hobbs, *Ancient Egypt: Everyday Life in the Land of the Nile*. New York: Sterling, 2013.

Rosalie David, *Handbook to Life in Ancient Egypt*. New York: Oxford University Press, 2008.

Adolf Erman, *Life in Ancient Egypt*. Translated by H.M. Tirard. Charleston, SC: Nabu, 2010.

Lucia Gahlin and Lorna Oakes, *Ancient Egypt*. London: Lorenz, 2013.

Zahi Hawass, *Pyramids: Treasures, Mysteries, and New Discoveries in Egypt*. New York: White Star, 2011.

Geoffrey Killen, *Egyptian Woodworking and Furniture*. Princes Risborough, UK: Shire, 2008.

Alfred Lucas and J.R. Harris, *Ancient Egyptian Materials and Industries*. New York: Dover, 2011.

William H. Peck, *The Material World of Ancient Egypt*. New York: Cambridge University Press, 2013.

Gay Robins, *The Art of Ancient Egypt*. Cambridge, MA: Harvard University Press, 2008.

Thomas Schneider, *Ancient Egypt: 101 Questions and Answers*. Ithaca, NY: Cornell University Press, 2013.

John M. White, *Everyday Life in Ancient Egypt*. New York: Dover, 2011.

Jim Whiting, *Life Along the Ancient Nile*. San Diego, CA: ReferencePoint Press, 2012.

Toby Wilkinson, *The Rise and Fall of Ancient Egypt*. New York: Random House, 2011.

Internet Sources

Sameh M. Arab, "Medicine in Ancient Egypt, Part 1," Arab World Books. www.arabworldbooks.com/articles8.htm.

André Dollinger, "Pharaonic Egypt: Law and Order," Ancient Egypt, July 2013. www.reshafim.org.il/ad/egypt/law_and_order.

Geraldine Pinch, "Ancient Egyptian Magic," BBC, February 17, 2011. www.bbc.co.uk/history/ancient/egyptians/magic_01.shtml.

Catharine H. Roehrig, "Egyptian Tombs," Metropolitan Museum of Art, October 2004. www.metmuseum.org/toah/hd/egtb/hd_egtb.htm.

Catherine Soubeyrand, "The Game of Senet," *Game Cabinet*, February 2013. www.gamecabinet.com/history/Senet.html.

Websites

Ancient Egypt Film Site (www.ancientegyptfilmsite.nl). This interesting and engaging site offers a list of more than eight hundred films and TV shows based on ancient Egypt and its culture. Each entry has its own separate page containing valuable information about the film.

Ancient Egypt Site (www.ancient-egypt.org). A Belgian Egyptologist's huge, handsomely mounted collection of web pages and links relating to ancient Egypt, including history, language, monuments, religion, and much more.

Egypt's Golden Empire, PBS (www.pbs.org/empires/egypt/newking dom/farming.html). With its usual attention to educating young people and the public in general, PBS supplies this excellent site on life in ancient Egypt.

Index

Picture Credits

About the Author

Historian and award-winning author Don Nardo has written numerous books about the ancient world, its peoples, and their cultures, including volumes on the Babylonians, Assyrians, Persians, Minoans, Greeks, Etruscans, Romans, and others. He is also the author of single-volume encyclopedias on ancient Mesopotamia, ancient Greece, ancient Rome, and Greek and Roman mythology. Nardo, who also composes and arranges orchestral music, lives with his wife, Christine, in Massachusetts.